IT'S A WORLD THING

GEOGRAPHY for Edexcel Specification B

REVISION

Bob Digby

Casimir Bowes-Jones

Russell Chapman

Stewart FitzGerald

Elizabeth Howard

OXFORD
UNIVERSITY PRESS

edexcel

OXFORD
UNIVERSITY PRESS

Great Clarendon Street, Oxford OX2 6DP

Oxford University Press is a department of the University of Oxford.
It furthers the University's objective of excellence in research,
scholarship, and education by publishing worldwide in

Oxford New York

Auckland Bangkok Buenos Aires Cape Town Chennai
Dar es Salaam Delhi Hong Kong Istanbul Karachi Kolkata
Kuala Lumpur Madrid Melbourne Mexico City Mumbai
Nairobi São Paulo Shanghai Taipei Tokyo Toronto

Oxford is a registered trade mark of Oxford University Press
in the UK and in certain other countries

© Bob Digby, Casimir Bowes-Jones, Russell Chapman, Stewart FitzGerald,
Elizabeth Howard 2004

The moral rights of the author have been asserted

Database right Oxford University Press (maker)

First published 2004

British Library Cataloguing in Publication Data

Data available

ISBN 0 19 913448 0

10 9 8 7 6 5 4 3 2 1

Printed and bound in Great Britain by Antony Rowe, Chippenham, Wiltshire.
Design and production by Hart McLeod, Cambridge.

Acknowledgements
Hand by Corbis/Dennis Scott
Onion by The Image Bank/Getty Images

Contents

Introduction

How to use this book

This book has been written to help you to revise for your geography GCSE. It has been written by teachers, with some input from their students, to help you to make sense of the course that you've been studying.

Before you begin, be clear about what this book is setting out to do. It is not a 'crammer's guide', which will try to tell you all you need to know in a few brief pages. We, the authors, chose not to do that, because:

a we don't know of any book which could do that for the course that you've been studying. Most revision guides deal with *themes*, such as population or industry. Your course is *issues-based*, about things that affect people and the environment they live in.

b your course has been designed to help you to understand geographical issues properly – not just rote-learn a few notes to get you through. We believe that, if you understand your course properly, you'll be able to handle any question that examiners give you.

The GCSE geography exams

What exams do I have to take?

Figure 1 below summarises what you have to do. To make sense of it, you need to know whether you are taking the Foundation level (where exams are coded 'F' below) or Higher level (where they are coded 'H').

Figure 1 Course summary

Exam papers/Coursework	Details	Marks	Time
Either Paper 1F (Foundation – grades C-G) **or** Paper 3H (Higher – grades A*-D)	A decision-making exercise based on pre-released resources issued to you during May	25%	1hour 15 minutes
Either Paper 2F (Foundation) **or** Paper 4H (Higher)	A written examination during June	50%	2 hours
Coursework	An investigation based on primary data	25%	Some time during the course

What do I have to know?

The course is divided up into units. **Core units** have to be studied by everyone. Figure 2 shows the core units (page references are given for this revision book).

Figure 2 Core units

Core units

Unit A1: Providing for population change

Population dynamics	See **Population dynamics** pages 47-54
Population and resources	See **Population and resources** pages 55-62

Unit A2: Planning for change

Settlement	See **Settlement** pages 15-22
Employment	See **Employment** pages 23-30

Unit A3: Coping with environmental change

Coasts	See **Coasts** pages 31-38
Hazards	See **Hazards** pages 39-46

These units will be examined by:
- ▉ the decision-making paper (paper 1F or 3H);
- ▉ section A of the written paper (paper 2F or 4H).

Whichever unit is examined in the decision-making paper will not be re-tested in the written paper. So, if Hazards is the topic for the decision-making paper, neither Coasts nor Hazards will be re-tested in paper 2F or 4H.

In addition, there are four option units, two of which you will have studied.

Figure 3 Option units

The option units address the theme of 'The use and abuse of the environment'.
You will have studied one of the B option units and one of the C option units.

Either		**And Either**	
Unit B4: Water	*See **Water** pages 63-70*	Unit C6: Farming	*See **Farming** pages 79-86*
Or		**Or**	
Unit B5: Weather and climate	*See **Weather and climate** pages 71-78*	Unit C7: Recreation and tourism	*See **Recreation and tourism** pages 87-94*

The option units will be examined in section B of the written paper (paper 2F or 4H). There will always be a question on the options you have studied.

Each unit in this revision book will give you precise guidance about the case studies and concepts which you will need to study for each topic. There are two things which you need to be aware of:

1   Each unit is divided into '*key questions*'. These are not questions which examiners will use exactly as they are written here, but they help examiners to know what kinds of things to ask you. They are questions to which you should have some kind of answer in your head, and also have an idea of what kinds of studies you have made to help answer them.

2   '*Focus case studies*' are those which **must** be studied in the unit. They are the **only** case studies which you may be asked to recall in the examination. For example, the unit on Coasts only requires you to study two case studies – one of a coast facing problems caused by erosion, and a second facing issues caused by development pressures. You don't need extra case studies. The examiners have done this so that you have a clear understanding of general concepts which is kept to a manageable level by limiting the places studied.

It will always help you to be able to refer to places you have studied in the exam, because credit is given for examples.

What shall I do with this book?

What we aim to do with this revision guide is help you with the revision process. The book won't cram the whole two-year course into one short guide, but it will help to develop your understanding as you work through it. While you use it, keep beside you:

a   the *It's a World Thing* student textbook, which has been written specifically for the GCSE you've been studying;

b   the work you've done in class and at home.

The exercises in this revision guide have been written to test you on knowledge and understanding, with some skills exercises such as using or drawing maps, graphs, and diagrams.

Revision is a personal thing!

Revision is possibly the hardest and most boring thing you will have to do. To make it work successfully, you need to make it manageable and fun!

Most current advice tells you to break everything down into small pieces / bitesizes. Our brains are so conditioned to watching commercial TV or listening to the radio that, in most cases, we only ever really concentrate for a few minutes at a time.

Consider why programme makers allow 12-15 minutes between adverts. It's just long enough to concentrate on what's going on. Now ask yourself how long you can concentrate in class; perhaps 15 minutes is about the best you can do there as well.

We have written this book to help you get the best out of a bad time, so get active and give this routine a whirl. It does work; it even helps time to pass remarkably quickly.

Don't try to revise for hours at a time!

Why kid yourself that you have learnt anything, just because you've been at it for so many hours? Most of the time you were daydreaming, with meaningless words floating across the page, or checking the clock to see how long it had been since you last had a break or a coffee (or played 'Solitaire', checked your e-mails, texted a friend, etc.).

Don't make loads of notes!

Some people will tell you to use index cards, so you can abbreviate your notes. But what is the point of that? The work in your book might already be brief enough, and possibly inaccurate abbreviations at that! Follow the activities in this book, which are designed to help you to learn **by understanding**.

Construct a timetable

Before you break for Easter, construct a revision timetable and allocate topics to slots:
- Every day has three sessions, but you should only use two of them.
- Each session comprises three units.

Build in breaks from work every day. You need to take time off and really get away from it all. Go for a run, bike ride, or to the cinema … clear your mind. Figure 4 shows the start of an example timetable.

Key: = free time

Figure 4 A revision timetable

	Monday	Tuesday	Wednesday	Thursday	Friday	Saturday	Sunday
9-12	Topic 1						
2-5		Topic 3					
7-10	Topic 2	Topic 4					

Get your files or books into order!

You need to do this before the Easter holidays as well. Make sure that you have everything in place.

Sort your files or exercise books along the lines of the specification	Arrange the contents of your files into the topics as they occur in the exam papers. Make sure that you know where the compulsory and options sections are.

Browse and cross-reference	Browse over everything and assess the scale of the task ahead. Have the *It's a World Thing* textbook and this revision guide at your side as you go through the topics for the first time. Add page references next to your work for easy checking later on.

Know your strongest and weakest topics

Prioritise revision topics according to your level of understanding	Make a list of your strongest and weakest areas, based on your marks or grades in homeworks, tests, mocks, etc. Know where the gaps are!

Allocate topics to your revision timetable	Make session 1 one of your strongest topics. You'll cover it quickly and feel more motivated. Then go to your weakest topic in the next session. Fill your schedule up in this way, balancing good with bad.

Add detail to your revision timetable

Based on your list of easy/strong topics and difficult/weak topics, fill in the details on your revision timetable. Allocate two slots for each topic, as illustrated in Figure 5.

Key:
R = revising-to-learn activities
T = testing-your-understanding activities

Figure 5 Completing the revision timetable

	Monday	Tuesday	Wednesday	Thursday	Friday	Saturday	Sunday
9-12	Topic 1 (easy) R		Topic 1 (easy) T				
2-5							
7-10							

Putting it all into action!

Revising-to-learn activities One hour at a time (1 unit)	For the first hour of the first session, read through the selected topic from your file and books. Copy out the sub-headings as you reach them, and leave spaces beneath each one. Using headings that you are already familiar with will help to reinforce your order of thinking. In the spaces you have created, pose your own questions from your notes and books, linking them to the relevant pages in this book. Think like an examiner. Test yourself. Try the 'what, where, why, how, consequences' routine each time, as shown in Figure 6 on page 9. Then have a few minutes off, before starting again on a related topic, or change subjects altogether but repeat this approach.

Testing-your-understanding activities	A day or two later, return to your sheets of sub-headings, questions and open spaces. Start to fill them in, without using your notes or books. Then complete the relevant pages in this book.
	See how much you can achieve. Don't worry about timing at this stage but do force yourself to write things down. Time will pass rapidly. Don't worry about the questions you can't answer.
	When you've finished, you'll have a good idea of what you really do know and what you don't! If you've filled in most of the gaps, you will feel good. If you've left gaps, you now know where they are, and they will be easy to look up because they are all in the same order as your files/books. Go back to these areas and read through them again.

Keep doing this until you've covered the entire contents of your course/exam papers.

By now, you will have created *summary* sheets of the topics, but in an active and testing manner. You won't have wasted time simply copying out your notes into new, reduced formats. You will have developed a *feel* for each topic and an order of ideas within each topic, which you can now take further.

What, where, why ...?

To help you prepare case studies in some detail, it is possible to use a formulaic approach. Most geographical case studies can be broken down into manageable portions that lead on from each other to build up the complete picture. This strategy can even get you out of a scrape in the exam room itself - if you are lost for content and organisation of ideas, just think what, where and why ...?

Figure 6 A framework for learning case studies

Case study	Population change in Malawi
What ...? Define the ISSUE that is being discussed in your example. This involves DESCRIPTION only and is a low-level but important skill.	**What is happening in Malawi?** Malawi has a youthful population, has experienced considerable growth, and is expected to grow from 10 million people in 2000 to 14 million by 2010. This reflects the role of women and has an impact on patterns of development.
Where ...? Draw a sketch map to show the location and learn basic details of distances, sizes and place names. This involves DESCRIPTION only and is again only a low-level skill, but it establishes evidence of your understanding.	**Where is Malawi and what is it like?** You could use the map from page 112 of the textbook and also sketch pyramid Figure 2. Malawi is an LEDC and has a typical population structure for a developing country: a high birth rate of 38 and a death rate of 22 per 1000, a low life expectancy (37 years), and high infant mortality (122 per 1000).
Why ...? Try to explain the reasons for the current situation. This should mean that you include some details about the **factors** which have allowed it to occur. This involves the use of geographic terminology and is a higher-level skill than description.	**Why is the population growing?** The birth rate is higher than the death rate because the use of medicines from aid programmes has reduced infant mortality, and vaccines/inoculations have forced back the age of death. Traditional customs, together with the status of women and value of children, mean that births have not yet fallen as quickly. Children remain assets and family size is still high, especially in rural areas.
How ...? Try to explain the causes of the current situation. This should mean that you include some details on the **processes** that have brought it about. This again involves the use of geographic terminology, and is a higher-level skill than description.	**How has Malawi's situation come about?** Malawi's youthful population structure is the reason why the population continues to grow. Children already born today are 'potential parents' of tomorrow, so children born 15 years ago are already on the verge of being parents. As infant mortality falls, more children survive to adulthood. As medical care and aid improves, life expectancy increases and, therefore, the total population grows.

Consequences ...?

Level 3 at GCSE involves you considering the after-effects of geographical events. Examiners assess your ability to use data to draw conclusions, and to explain how ordinary events become serious issues.

You can **SEE** your way to success by thinking in terms of the following obvious consequences:

• **S**ocial - how people's lives are changed in both positive and negative senses.

• **E**conomic - the way the local/national economy changes; positive and negative multiplier effects.

• **E**nvironmental – the positive and negative impacts on the local and wider environments.

What are the consequences for Malawi?

Continued high rates of population growth put pressure on resources and can reinforce the conditions of poverty. Population growth can be seen as a symptom of poverty - because low levels of welfare and economic well-being make children **assets** to families in both the short and the long term. Young family members help to bring up the babies, work the land and act as support to elderly parents where no pensions exist.

Socially. Family size is decided at a local level and will lead to a growing population as more babies survive into parenthood - more hands to work but more mouths to feed!

Economically. The workforce grows, but the amount of wealth generated has to be shared among more people. Relative poverty increases.

Environmentally. More land has to be used to feed the population and this can result in the overuse of poorer lands if the best land has already been used for other purposes. If crops fail, the land may suffer desertification and people will be forced to migrate to the cities in the hope of survival.

Testing your understanding

Visual notes and spider diagrams	Now start all over again, but this time select a topic and create spider diagrams based only on the things you have remembered which are related to that topic. Again, go for the 'what, where, why ...?' sequence.
	Then compare the spider diagrams with the information in your book or file and draw improved versions.
	Draw diagrams of key features and test yourself on annotations.

Having got this far, you are now ready to try out a few timed exercises, old exam papers and the work your teachers asked you to do. The problem with these things is that you will not know if you are right or wrong until you get back to school! So leave them until the last few days of the holidays. By then you should be more competent and confident anyway. Better to return to school with a degree of confidence, or at least a list of questions that you need to ask, than an exercise you did three weeks earlier.

Getting through the DME

This paper is based on the idea that you can make a decision about a problem or issue from a number of options, for which there are proposed solutions. The exam itself:

a   consists of structured questions, ranging from short answers (worth 1-3 marks) to one final question which requires extended writing and is worth about 12 marks. If you are taking the Foundation paper, the longer 12-mark questions will be split up into shorter questions worth fewer marks each.

b   assesses one of the core units A1-A3.

c   is based upon resource materials, in the form of a booklet, which you will receive about three weeks before the exam. You will get a copy *before* the exam and an original, high-quality copy *during* the exam. You can't take written notes into the exam with you.

d   supposes that you will spend lesson and homework time in preparing for the exam by reading and analysing the resource booklet.

How will I know what to do?

Remember the 4 R's – Read, Recognise, Reconstruct, and Review.

Read!

Check out what you know. Find out what you don't.

Check through the copy of the resources you've been given. Highlight the words you don't know the meaning of, or phrases you don't understand. What are the key words and definitions that you need to know? Use Figure 7 to compile a list here as you go.

Figure 7 File of key words and phrases

Term	Definition
1.	
2.	
3.	
4.	
5.	
6.	
7.	
8.	
9.	
10.	
11.	
12.	
13.	
14.	
15.	
16.	

Recognise!

This is about recognising how the resources fit with the course you've been studying. Read the resources and ask yourself the following questions:

1 Do I know what the problem is about?
2 How does it fit in with the course that I've been doing?
3 Which core unit is it testing?
4 What knowledge and revision will help me to understand the problem or issue more clearly?

Be sure that you also know the answers to these questions:

5 What resources have I been given about the place, the problem, and the causes of the problem?
6 What resources have I been given about the effects of the problem?
7 What possibilities are there for solving the problem?
8 And, of course, what decision will I have to make?

Reconstruct!

This stage involves you taking each of the resources stage by stage. Consider the following questions:

1 What is this place like?
2 What are the issues affecting the place?
3 Who is involved? How and why are they involved?
4 What is causing the problem? How have these causes arisen?
5 What impacts is the problem having? Upon whom is it having impacts?
6 What are the proposed solutions to the problem?
7 What are the implications of each solution, if it were to be adopted?
8 What are the costs and benefits of each proposal?
9 Are there conflicts involved in each proposal? Would a conflict matrix help?

To help you through this process, copy out and try some of the exercises in Figures 8-11 below on some spare paper.

1 What is this place like?
2 What are the issues affecting the place?
3 Who is involved? How and why are they involved?
4 What is causing the problem? How have these causes arisen?
5 What impacts is the problem having? Upon whom is it having impacts?

Figure 8 Analysing the issue

Make sure that you are clear about what each of the proposed solutions involves doing.

Figure 9 Analysing the proposals

	Social impacts	Economic impacts	Environmental impacts
Scheme 1			
Scheme 2			
Scheme 3			
Scheme 4			
Scheme 5			

Figure 10 Analysing the costs and benefits of each proposal

	Costs	Benefits
Scheme 1		
Scheme 2		
Scheme 3		
Scheme 4		
Scheme 5		

You can use a conflict matrix **either**:
- to show how different people might be in conflict, and why; **or**
- whether different solutions are in conflict with each other, and why.

Figure 11 A conflict matrix

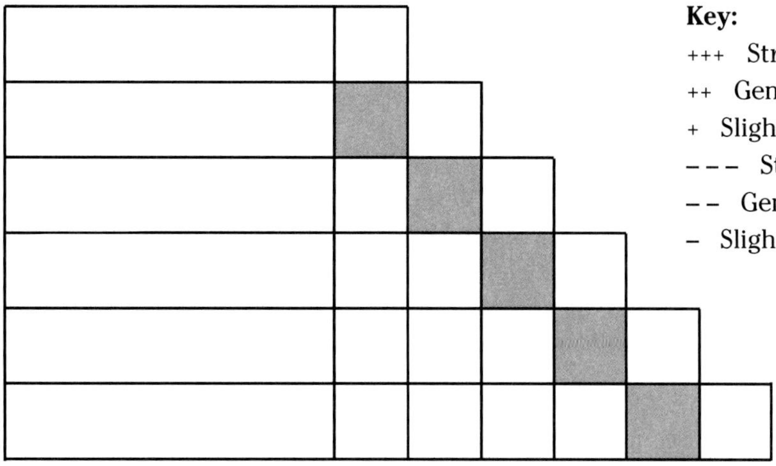

Key:
+++ Strong agreement
++ General agreement
+ Slight agreement
– – – Strong disagreement
– – Generally disagreement
– Slight disagreement

Review!

This stage involves you in reaching a decision, after reviewing all the material you've studied.

1 Review each of the proposed solutions and your analysis of each one.
2 Which solution seems to be the 'best' and why? Is there one single solution, or would a combination of more than one solution work best?
3 Which solution is the weakest? Why?
4 Can you write a detailed account, saying why you support one or two of the proposed solutions?
5 Can you conclude by saying why you rejected the others?

If you can do this, you've prepared yourself thoroughly for the exam! Good luck!

Getting through papers 2F/4H

Most of this revision book is about the content which you'll be tested on for this exam paper. Below are some of the basic details about this paper.

The sections

There are two sections, A and B. You should answer **all** parts of section A, which will cover the core units (see below). However, look carefully at the choices in section B. You have to do **one of** *either* Water *or* Weather and climate, and **one of** *either* Farming *or* Recreation and tourism.

Be smart and answer the questions on the units you have been studying! You are guaranteed a question on each of the options you have been studying, so don't blow it by answering the wrong questions!

Section A will test the core units of:
A1 Population dynamics, and Population and resources
A2 Settlement, and Employment
A3 Coasts, and Hazards

Section A will contain two questions. These questions will test those core units which are **NOT** tested in Papers 1F or 3H (the DME). So, if the DME is about Employment, then neither Employment nor Settlement will be tested in section A of Papers 2F or 4H. In this case, you would be *guaranteed* questions on Coasts, Hazards, and Population.

Timing

Timing is crucial to gain the maximum marks.

Each question in **section A**:
- counts for 30 marks, i.e. 60 in total. Allow 60% of the time for this section, i.e. 72 minutes. That's 36 minutes per question. Don't over-run!
- consists of structured questions, ranging from short answers worth 2 marks to those requiring extended writing, worth about 8-9 marks. The longest answers will demand case-study knowledge.

In **section B**:
- each question counts for 20 marks, i.e. 40 in total. You need to allow 40% of the time for this section, i.e. 48 minutes. That's 24 minutes per question. Again, don't over-run!
- you will meet structured questions again, ranging from short answers worth 2 marks to those requiring extended writing, worth about 6 marks. The longest answers will demand case-study knowledge.

GOOD LUCK!

Settlement

What do I have to know?

The Settlement unit has three guiding questions for study:

2.1 Where shall we build new homes?

2.2 How is rapid growth affecting cities in LEDCs?

2.3 Can urban areas be made more sustainable?

Each is split into key questions (a), (b), and (c) below, and these determine what you must know and understand.

2.1 Where shall we build new homes?

Key questions	What you have to know and understand
a How is demand for housing growing?	■ **Know** the reasons for this growth in demand. ■ **Understand** why this demand varies from one part of the UK to another. ■ **Understand** the issues surrounding the need to meet demand for new housing.
b Should we build on greenfield or brownfield sites?	■ **Know** the difference between a greenfield and a brownfield site. ■ **Understand** the advantages and disadvantages of choosing either option. ■ **Understand** the implications for building more developments on greenfield sites, for example, through increased urban sprawl, loss of agricultural land and pressures at the rural-urban fringe.

The specification states that you must have studied generally about greenfield and brownfield issues, but case studies about such developments are not required for the exam.

2.2 How is rapid growth affecting cities in LEDCs?

Key questions	What you have to know and understand
a Why are cities in LEDCs growing so fast?	■ **Know** the reasons for this rapid growth, i.e. natural increase and rural-urban migration. ■ **Know and understand** how rural-urban migration is often the result of a changing rural economy.
b What are the effects of such rapid urban growth?	■ **Know and understand** the opportunities and problems created by such rapid growth, e.g. housing, services, employment and quality of life.
c How can we improve quality of life in squatter settlements?	■ **Know** the meaning and characteristics of a squatter settlement. ■ **Know and understand** how squatter settlements change over time, e.g. as they become more established. ■ **Know and understand** a scheme put into action in an LEDC city to improve the overall quality of life, *either* by individuals (self-help) *or* by city authorities.

The specification states that you must have studied a named LEDC city. It is possible (or even better!) to study all three key questions above with reference to the same city. You must especially know **one** scheme to improve the overall quality of life for inhabitants of squatter settlements.

2.3 Can urban areas be made more sustainable?

Key questions	What you have to know and understand
a Can we solve urban traffic problems?	■ **Understand** the meaning of sustainable with regard to urban areas. ■ **Know and understand** the variety of traffic problems in an urban area, and how they can be resolved.
b How should we deal with waste?	■ **Understand** why waste is a problem for urban areas. ■ **Know and understand** the roles of individuals and organizations in dealing with waste. ■ **Understand** the advantages and disadvantages of dealing with waste sustainably, e.g. through recycling and reducing waste.

The specification states that you must have studied a waste and traffic management scheme in a named town or city. They can be two different cities or the same; they can be in either an LEDC or an MEDC, or can be a mixture of both. You could even use cities you have studied in other units from the course.

Where to build new homes

The following material refers to pages 6-13 in the *It's a World Thing* student textbook.

Before you start the main revision activities, try this quick quiz:

1 Which is growing more quickly – the UK's population or its demand for housing?
2 Define the term brownfield site.
3 In which county is Ashford?
4 What's a transport corridor? What is its link to urban development?

Revision activities

1 The number of households in the UK is growing at a much faster rate than the population. You can see this on page 6 of the textbook (Figure 2).
  a What are the reasons for this?
  b How is this contributing to a housing crisis?
  c Which parts of the UK are most affected by this housing shortage and why?
2 Write down definitions of a brownfield and a greenfield site.
3 Now study the following list of statements about building housing on greenfield or brownfield sites (Figure 1), and decide whether each is an advantage or a disadvantage, and whether it refers to a greenfield or a brownfield site.

Figure 1

a An infrastructure may already exist, e.g. electricity, water, sewerage.	**g** The sites are often small in size.	**l** There may be little open space for leisure.
b They are cheaper to develop.	**h** They are much more accessible by car and public transport.	**m** Countryside is accessible easily.
c Loss of agricultural land may be a problem.	**i** Land prices are cheaper.	**n** Protests are likely from local residents.
d Land on sites such as these is expensive.	**j** Work is much closer for people.	**o** Commuting takes longer.
e They can lead to pressure on the rural-urban fringe.	**k** Leisure in cities is more accessible, e.g. theatres, clubs, restaurants.	**p** Not all towns have these sites available.
f They can increase building densities.		

What's a NIMBY? • What's the link between demand for housing and quarries in the countryside?

The effects of urban growth on Ashford

Study Figure 2, showing the south-easterly part of Ashford. To locate it, look at Figure 4 on page 9 of the textbook. This activity is designed to help you to understand greenfield issues.

Figure 2 South-eastern Ashford

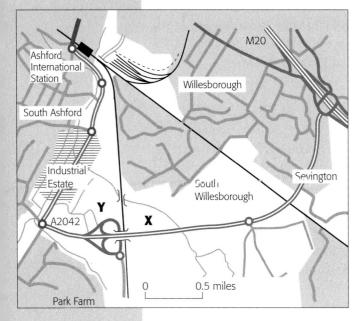

Revision activities

1 Point X on the map marks the spot for a proposed new housing estate.
  a Why would this be a good place for a new housing development?
  b Suggest three positive impacts which this housing development could have for Ashford.
  c Suggest three negative impacts which this development could have for the town.
2 What might residents of nearby South Willesborough have to say about the proposal?
3 a A town like Ashford has few brownfield sites. Suggest reasons why.
  b What implications does this have for meeting housing demand in the future?
4 Ashford Borough Council has suggested building a car park for a Park and Ride scheme at Point Y on the map.
  a What is a Park and Ride scheme?
  b Why is Point Y a suitable choice for this?
  c Why is this scheme a sustainable option?

Brownfield sites

The Millennium Dome at Greenwich in London was built on a 120-hectare derelict site surrounded on three sides by the River Thames. It was the site of a former gasworks, abandoned for over 20 years. The site was polluted and had to be decontaminated before any building could begin.

Revision activities

1 What arguments might planners put forward for building the Dome on a brownfield site, rather than on a greenfield site on the edge of the city?
2 What positive environmental impacts can brownfield developments such as the Millennium Dome have on the surrounding area?
3 'Green spaces are limited in built-up areas. It would be far better to have created an urban park than the Millennium Dome, and cheaper too.' How far do you agree with this view?
4 Read pages 10-13 of the textbook, which summarise the issues about greenfield and brownfield sites in Ashford. In 100 words, summarise:
  a why brownfield sites are not always the solution to the UK's housing problems;
  b why greenfield site developments raise protests from local people.

What's more sustainable – brownfield or greenfield? • Can a greenfield site ever represent sustainable development?

How rapid growth affects LEDC cities

The following material refers to pages 14-21 in the student textbook.

Why are LEDC cities growing?

Pages 16-21 in the textbook look at São Paulo, a very large city in south-east Brazil. You may have studied another city; if you have, substitute São Paulo in the questions below with the name of the city you have looked at.

Revision activities

Study Figure 3 below, which shows details of people's lives from a village in Peru. Who is likely to stay in the village? Who might be tempted to move to the nearest large city? People's lives depend on personal experience, so decide whether these people are likely to move, or not.

1 Draw a table on A4 paper with three columns. List the eight names from Figure 3 in the first column and then head the second column 'Reasons to move', and the third 'Reasons to stay'. Consider all eight people and:
   a write down reasons which might encourage them to move away to the city; and
   b reasons why they might stay put in the village.
2 Go through your list and:
   a tick those reasons to leave which are push factors, 'pushing' people away from the rural area;
   b place a cross beside those that are 'pull' factors, attracting people to the city;
   c compare your list with Figures 3 and 4 on page 15 of the textbook.

Figure 3 Eight scenarios for rural-urban migration

Juan: Male, aged 14. Abandoned by his mother and raised by his older sister in return for working at home. No schooling. Family has very low income.	**Rosa**: Female aged 12. She is the eldest of 5 children and has had 6 years of primary schooling. Her family owns 5 hectares of good-quality land.	**Marco**: Male, aged 25. He has 4 years of primary schooling and is married with 3 children. He is a farmer and shares 8 hectares of family land with his father. Above-average income.	**Ana**: Female, aged 23. She had some secondary schooling and worked as a maid in a city, but now has a baby. She has 6 younger brothers and sisters and a father who is unable to work. The family has a little land, of poor quality, bringing in a low income.
Pedro: Male, aged 26 He had 2 years of primary schooling. He is married with 4 children, 3 of whom are at school (for which the family has to pay). He earns little from the family's small landholding, and has to have an extra job. The family income is low.	**Celia**: Female, aged 31. She had 6 years of primary schooling. She now has 10 children, of whom 7 are at school. Her husband is an electrician who works and lives away from home in a city 100 km away. As a result of his job, the family has above-average income.	**Maria**: Female aged 37. She had 4 years of primary schooling. Her husband died recently and she has 4 children, all married (three living locally). She has 5 hectares of land, some of which she rents out. She has average income, helped by her family when needed.	**Maro**: Male, aged 17. He is the eldest in a large family, and has had 9 years of schooling. His father works in a city 180 km away, and he has other relations there. The family wants him to train as a mechanic, then go to college to become an engineer.

Push-pull – what's the difference? • How do squatters get to be permanent residents?

Urban growth in LEDCs

This page is about the effects of rapid growth in cities such as São Paulo. Take 10 minutes to read pages 18-19 of the textbook and study the photographs. Close the book and try these activities.

Revision activities: Test your memory!

1 **a** What is São Paulo's population?
   b What is the name given to squatter settlements on the outskirts of the city?
   c What is the difference between formal and informal employment?
   d Name three jobs typical of the informal employment in such cities.

2 What would you say are the positive and negative features of living in a favela? Make a copy of Figure 4 to help you.

3 Why is it in the interests of (**a**) residents and (**b**) the city authorities to improve squatter settlements?

Figure 4

	+ve	–ve
Employment		
Housing		
Quality of life		
Services available		

Quality of life in the favelas

Quality of life varies considerably in LEDC cities. Wealth determines not only where you live but also your prospects for the future. Read pages 20-21 of the textbook, then close the book and do the following activities.

Revision activities

1 Make a large A4-sized copy of Figure 5 to complete from memory.

Figure 5

Who?	In which areas of the city do they live?	What is their quality of life like now?	What is their quality of life likely to be like in ten years time?
The wealthy			
Middle/low income families with permanent work			
Low/no income families - out of work or relying on informal work			

2 Using your completed copy of Figure 5, explain why there is an increasing gap between rich and poor in LEDC cities.

3 Several attempts have been made to improve the quality of life and the environment for those living in favelas. Compare *low-cost improvements* and *self-help schemes* using the 'who, what, where, how' approach.
   - Who is it for?
   - What does it consist of?
   - Where in the city?
   - What has to happen to bring this about?
   - What are the social, economic and environmental consequences (in local and wider contexts)?

Is self-help the same as DIY? • Why are there few or no paved roads in the favelas?

Making urban areas sustainable

The following material refers to pages 22-29 in the student textbook.

Solving the traffic problem

Before you start this exercise, try this quick quiz:

1 Why aren't cars a sustainable form of transport? Give five reasons.
2 Which fuel is best - petrol, diesel or LPG? What are the alternatives?
3 What is 'landfill'?
4 Are reducing, recycling, repairing and re-using possible?

The amount of traffic generally, and in cities specifically, has increased well beyond the rate of population growth – as shown in Figure 6. The impacts on people and the environment have been considerable. Read pages 24-25 in the textbook to find out how and why this is the case.

Figure 6 The growth in vehicle numbers in the UK

	Population	Vehicles
1960	52 million	5 million
2000	60 million	28 million
Increase	15%	460%

Revision activities

1 Use Figure 6 to draw a line graph which shows the increase in population and vehicle numbers between 1960 and 2000.
2 Figure 7 shows ten criteria for sustainable development. Make an A4-sized copy of the table and complete it as follows:
   a In the 'Yes/no' column, say whether the use of cars or lorries for journeys helps to create sustainable development.
   b In the 'Because?' column, explain why you have said 'yes' or 'no'.

Figure 7 Ten criteria for sustainability

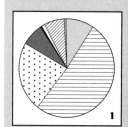

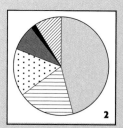

Criteria for sustainability	Yes/no	Because?
Financially viable		
Environmentally friendly in its building materials and design.		
Minimises adverse impacts on nearby residents.		
Protects and encourages native vegetation.		
Minimises waste.		
Encourages recycling.		
Minimises energy use.		
Is inclusive, i.e. benefits and includes people from across all communities.		
Is affordable, within financial reach of everyone.		
Minimises pollution.		

☐ car
☐ tube
☐ surface rail
☐ bus
■ pedal bike
☐ motor bike
▨ walk
☐ other specify

Figure 8

3 Study Figure 8, showing how people get to work in two different parts of London in 2004. Which graph (1 or 2) shows a more sustainable environment, and why?
4 In 2003, London introduced a congestion charge for vehicles entering the CBD between 7am and 6.30pm. How does this compare with Boston's approach to traffic management, on pages 26-7 of the textbook?

Congestion charging, higher petrol tax, motorway tolls – name four other ways of reducing private motor traffic on the road.

How to deal with waste

What happens to London's waste?

Before doing the activities on this page you should study pages 28-29 of the textbook. Because this is a case study, take 10-15 minutes to study London's waste problems and then close the book. Try to remember key data and the key ideas about how waste might be managed in future.

Revision activities

1 Which percentage option in Figure 9 fits which treatment process for different types of waste in London?

Figure 9

	Which %?	**Choose from**
Landfill site in London		1%, 10%, 12%, 17% and 60%
Landfill site outside London		
Composting		
Recycling		
Energy from waste		

2 **a** Why is this a problem for (**i**) London and (**ii**) counties surrounding London?
  b Match which proportion of all waste going outside London goes to which county in Figure 10.

3 Every means of collecting waste has its problems. In your notebook, give two problems for each of the following ways of collecting and transporting waste in London:
  a 500 waste-collection vehicles
  b 45 civic-amenity sites
  c 2 energy-from-waste plants
  d 3 landfill sites

Figure 10

	Which %?	**Choose from**
Bedfordshire		8%, 8%, 8%, 8%, 13%, 22% and 33%
Berkshire		
Buckinghamshire		
Essex		
Hertfordshire		
Kent		
Oxfordshire		

4 What are (**a**) the practical, and (**b**) the ethical issues of trying to persuade regions outside London to take its waste?

5 Make a large A4-sized copy of Figure 11. It shows four options for the future as far as waste management is concerned. It assumes that present levels of waste generation are not sustainable. Consider recycling first. On the diagram:
  a complete the box 'How can this be made to work?';
  b complete the box 'What attitudes need to change?';
  c repeat the exercise for the other three options.

6 What kinds of changes have to occur before London can cope with its waste in a sustainable way?

Figure 11 Waste – options for the future

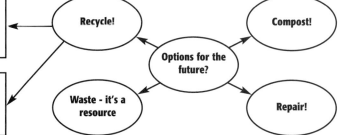

How can this be made to work?

What attitudes need to change?

Recycle! — Compost! — Options for the future? — Waste - it's a resource — Repair!

Sustainability depends upon us all adopting the 4Rs; what are they?

What words do I have to know?

There is no set list of words in the specification that you must know. However, examiners will know that you have probably used the set textbook, and will feel free to use some or all of the following words in the examinations:

affordable housing	conurbation	greenfield site	NIMBYism	rural-urban fringe	sustainable development
brownfield site	counter-urbanisation	landfill	push-and-pull factors	rural-urban migration	transport corridor
car pooling	favela	migrant	quality of life	self-help housing	urban renewal
commuter	formal and informal employment	CBD	rural	squatter settlement	urbanisation

The glossary in the student textbook will help you with the meanings of these words and phrases.

What other sources can help me?

Using the student textbook will give you enough material to take you to the highest grades. However, if you did not study cities in the textbook, here are some websites to give you background material on other case studies.

General urban issues

Geotopics web page http://www.bennett.karoo.net/topics/urban.html has a good selection of urban links and themes.

BBC's GCSE Bitesize web page for Geography http://www.bbc.co.uk/schools/gcsebitesize/geography/cities/index.shtml has great links to urban themes, together with self-testing facility.

Greenfield and brownfield sites in MEDCs

Friends of the Earth web page http://www.foe.co.uk contains a range of reports about housing, and has a web search facility for, e.g. 'brownfield' or 'greenfield'.

Urban issues in LEDCs

The Global eye website has material on urban issues in LEDCs, e.g. Rio's 'Favela-Barrio' programme. The Spring 2004 edition on global cities is brilliant! Go to http://www.globaleye.org.uk and follow links to 'back issues'.

Waste and traffic management

http://www.dft.gov.uk/ is the UK government web page for transport issues.

Video

- ■ BBC Video series 'World 2000' Programme 4 Urbanisation.
- ■ Brazil 2000 – Programme 1 'City : Rio de Janeiro' and Programme 4 'Work: Sao Paulo'.
- ■ GCSE Bitesize Revision (1999) contains an overview of urban themes, targeted at this age range. It explores city growth and quality of life (30 minutes each).

Try these questions

1   For **either** a greenfield **or** a brownfield development that you have studied, describe how the site has been used to allow the city/region to expand, and what conflicts it has caused. (*9 marks*)

2   For an LEDC city that you have studied, describe how and why its population has expanded, and how well it has been able to cope with increased numbers of people. (*9 marks*)

Employment

What do I have to know?

The Employment unit has two guiding questions for study:

2.4 How is the global workplace changing?

2.5 What is the impact of new job opportunities in MEDCs?

Each is split into the key questions (a) to (d) below, and these determine what you must know and understand.

2.4 How is the global workplace changing?

Key questions	What you have to know and understand
a How have employment patterns changed?	■ **Know** the different sectors of employment – primary, secondary, tertiary and quaternary. ■ **Know** about the shift from primary to secondary and tertiary jobs over time. ■ **Understand** how employment structure changes as a result of economic development.
b What are TNCs and where do they operate?	■ **Know** what is meant by the term 'TNC'. ■ **Know** how TNCs grow and develop. ■ **Understand** why the locations of TNC headquarters and manufacturing sites tend to be different.
c What are the impacts for a host country?	■ **Know and understand** the advantages and disadvantages of a TNC to a host country and to its employees.
d How are campaigns used?	■ **Know and understand** reasons for a campaign against either child labour or unfair trade, and what it has done to try to raise awareness, raise funds and lobby politicians to try to bring about change.

The specification states that you must have studied a named TNC. The examples in the *It's a World Thing* student textbook are Ford and Nike.

2.5 What is the impact of new job opportunities in MEDCs?

Key questions	What you have to know and understand
a Where are the new jobs?	■ **Know** about 'new employment' and be able to give examples and locations where it has grown. ■ **Know and understand** the growth of employment opportunities at the urban-rural fringe.
b What are the advantages of the rural-urban fringe for businesses?	■ **Understand** the advantages of accessibility and land availability to companies.
c How has this changed the urban-rural fringe?	■ **Understand** how changes occur to land use, transport infrastructure and urban sprawl.
d How might central business districts fight back?	■ **Know and understand** the decline in shopping and employment opportunities. ■ **Understand** the role of local authorities in bringing about change and invigorating local economies. ■ **Understand** the response of local authorities and businesses to attract jobs and customers back.

The specification states that you must have studied changing employment in one named town/city in an **MEDC**. The example used in the textbook is Reading.

Different types of employment

The following material refers to pages 30-41 in the *It's a World Thing* student textbook.

How and why are jobs changing?

Before you start the main revision activities, try this quick quiz:

1 Describe what is meant by:
- **a** primary, secondary, tertiary and quaternary employment;
- **b** formal and informal economy;
- **c** MEDC, LEDC, NIC.

Revision activities

1 Study Figure 1 below, which classifies employment.
- **a** Match the employment types in Column A with their definitions in Column C, and then add the correct identification letters to Column B.
- **b** Add three examples of each type of employment in Column D.

Figure 1

A Employment types	B	C Definitions	D Examples
Primary		(a) Manufacturing goods using raw materials	Primary =
Secondary		(b) Hi-tech or highly specialised and trained employment	Secondary =
Tertiary		(c) Based around production of raw materials	Tertiary =
Quaternary		(d) Service employment	Quaternary =

2 The two right-hand columns of Figure 2 show the percentage of people employed in each sector in an MEDC and LEDC, *but in the wrong order*. Place the percentages in the correct order in the two left-hand columns. One has been done for you.

3 a Draw two pie charts to show the pattern of employment in an MEDC and an LEDC. Don't forget to add the key!
b List **three** differences between the employment structures of MEDCs and LEDCs.

4 In Figure 3 below, match each statement about employment with one of the reasons on the right. Write the correct reason letter in the centre column.

Figure 2

	MEDC	LEDC	Select from MEDC	Select from LEDC
Primary	2		42	28
Secondary			2	54
Tertiary			56	18

Figure 3

Statement		Reason
Many LEDCs have a high percentage of workers in the primary sector.		(a) Cheap labour and available raw materials.
Most LEDCs have a growing secondary sector.		(b) Many work on the land as subsistence farmers.
MEDCs have a small primary sector.		(c) Competition from cheaper goods from abroad.
Most MEDCs have a decreasing secondary sector.		(d) Increasing demand for services.
MEDCs tend to have a large tertiary sector.		(e) Increasing machinery on farms.

Primary jobs are usually the best paid. True or false? • Research and development is an example of quaternary work. True or false?

Globalisation

This material focuses on Ford and refers to pages 34-37 in the *It's a World Thing* student textbook.

How do TNCs grow and develop?

Read pages 34-37 in the textbook and then try this quick quiz. The questions are about Ford, so you should change them if you've used another case study.

1 What is a TNC?
2 What is meant by globalisation?
3 Where is Ford's headquarters?
4 Name some countries where Ford vehicles are manufactured.
5 Where are Mondeo engines made?
6 Where does the assembly of the Mondeo take place?
7 Why is there a difference in the answers to questions 5 and 6?

Revision activities

The 'Ford 2000' initiative was set up in 1995. This policy of global development aimed to produce cars to appeal to a worldwide market. Spend 15 minutes reading and thinking about the textbook pages again, so you understand why Ford is such a large company and how and why Ford decided to invest in India.

1 look at the statements in Figure 4 and:
   a give reasons for each statement;
   b explain the benefit(s) for Ford of each statement;
   c explain the benefit(s) for India if Ford's plan works.
2 How successful do you think the Ford 2000 initiative has been? What evidence is there to support your answer?
3 Why did Ford see India as a worthwhile nation to invest in? Use the following sub-titles to construct your answer.
   - The size of India's economy.
   - The size of India's population.
   - The structure of India's population.
   - Labour costs in India.
   - The desire for expansion into the Asian-Pacific region.
4 Ford used several strategies to present a positive image in India. Copy Figure 5 below into your notebooks and complete it.

Figure 4

- Growth of the company will occur.
- Cars will be produced for a worldwide market.
- Production costs will be reduced.
- India is a huge (and fairly untapped) market.
- A global presence will be established.

Figure 5

	What Ford did	How it helps the company	How Ford believe that it helps their workforce
Organisation structure			
Employment structure			
Decision making			
Training of employees			
In-service training			

Ford, Jaguar, Land Rover, Volvo – Why did Ford want all of these brand names? ● India's middle classes are the same size as those of the EU. T or F?

The impact of TNCs on host countries

This material focuses on Nike and refers to pages 38-41 in the textbook.

Before you start the main revision activities, try this quick quiz. The questions are about Nike, so you should change them if you've used another case study.

1 Where is Nike's headquarters? What does the company produce?

2 Name three countries where Nike has manufacturing functions?

3 Name the production costs of this product, e.g. shipping and labour.

4 Name the costs to the retailer, e.g. advertising.

5 Why is there such a big difference between the production costs of a pair of Nike trainers and the cost to the consumer?

Revision activities

Consider the advantages/disadvantages which TNCs can bring to their host nations, i.e. those countries in which they locate. Read pages 38-41 in the textbook and do the following questions.

1 Ten statements are listed in Figure 6 about the advantages and disadvantages which TNCs bring to their host countries. However, they've been mixed up.

Figure 6

- Businesses are set up which the host country may not otherwise have.
- Any jobs created are often poorly paid and exploit local workers.
- TNCs act on their own behalf and profits are sent out of the host country.
- Better transport links and medical and education services may be established in the host country.
- Only a limited range of products is actually exported. The decisions are made by the TNC and not by the host country.
- Employment is created in the host country.
- The economy of the host country is improved.
- TNCs often only stay for a short period before closing down and moving to another host country, if the currency strengthens and production becomes cheaper elsewhere.
- Exports to worldwide markets are increased.
- Neither safety records nor environmental sensitivity have always been good.

  a Classify the ten statements into either advantages or disadvantages, using a larger copy of Figure 7.

  b Then add two more advantages and two more disadvantages of your own to complete the table.

Figure 7

Advantages	Disadvantages
1	
2	

2 A pair of Nike 'Air Pegasus' training shoes costs about $70 in the USA. Figure 3 on page 39 of the textbook shows the breakdown of this amount.

  a What *proportion* of the $70 goes to: **i** Nike; **ii** Nike's producers; **iii** retailers?

  b At which stages of the process is most value added to the trainers?

  c Who are the winners and losers of this process?

  d How have such figures led to criticism of Nike?

3 **a** Name three groups which campaign *against* Nike.

  b What are the strengths of their arguments?

  c What are the weaknesses of their arguments?

  d Which groups are they attempting to help the most?

4 From your research and study, how successful would you say that these campaigns have been?

Are TNCs exploiters of both local labour and the host nation? • What would TNCs say?

New jobs in an MEDC

Reading is a good example of the regeneration of a town or city in an MEDC, both:

■ economically – because it is part of the M4 corridor, which has generated huge economic growth in south-east England; and

■ environmentally – because the urban environment has altered considerably on the outskirts and in the centre.

Use the following activities to help you understand how and why this regeneration has taken place. Use pages 44-45 of the *'It's a World Thing'* student textbook to help you.

Revision activities

1 Copy Figure 8 into your notebooks with plenty of space in the boxes and use the textbook to draw a *simple* sketch of Reading in the large central box.

2 Give grid references for each of the places named around the outside of the central box. Then close the textbook.

3 Now draw arrows to connect each outer box to the correct location on your sketch.

4 Add detail to the outer boxes (a maximum of 10 words per box). Useful phrases or words to use are: accessibility, range of jobs, new shopping centre, light manufacture, distribution/call centre, comfortable workplace, pedestrianisation.

Figure 8 Reading

| Broad Street in town centre | Green Park Business Estate | Thames Valley Business Park |

| | | Reading Railway Station |

| | | The Oracle Centre |

| | | Reading International Business Park |

| Brunel Retail & Reading Link Retail Parks | Madejski Stadium | A33 Relief Road |

Out-of-town developments

Why does out-of-town development take place? Read pages 46-51 of the textbook to help you understand what has happened in Reading, and why.

The bid-rent theory

1 Figure 9 shows a graph outline to represent what happens to the cost of land as you move away from a city or town centre.

   a Copy the graph outline into your notebooks and label the axes.

   b Then draw the curve to show the pattern of land costs as you move out of the CBD.

   c Finally, annotate the curve to explain what happens to the cost of land in relation to distance from the CBD, and why.

2 Much development has taken place on the outskirts of Reading. Make a large copy of Figure 10 to describe what has happened to four human activities in Reading and why.

3 The new out-of-town developments meant that Reading's CBD struggled to compete. Read pages 50-51 of the textbook and think about how Reading dealt with this problem. Then use the information in the first two columns of Figure 11 to complete the third column.

Figure 9 A bid-rent curve

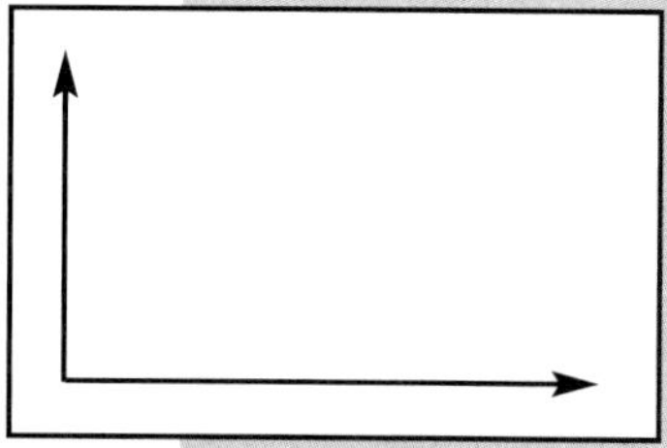

Figure 10

	What has happened?	Examples in Reading	Why has this happened?
Retail and shopping			
Employment			
Roads			
Leisure and sporting activities			

Figure 11

Problem trends in the CBD	What could local planners do to reverse these trends?	What did Reading's planners actually do to tackle the problems?
1 Many shops are vacant and the CBD is now perceived as unattractive.	■ Redevelop the area: **a** pedestrianise the retail zone; **b** improve the environment of the CBD.	
2 The environmental quality has been reduced, leading to reduced sales in shops.	■ Redevelop the CBD into 'mall-style' shopping centres.	
3 As a result, there is reduced income from shop rents and sales.	■ Regenerate older buildings and alter how existing buildings are used.	
4 The CBD has become a zone of estate agents, charity shops and cheap 'Poundstretcher' retailers.	■ Improve the reputation of the CBD by attracting big name stores, such as Harvey Nichols. ■ Extend the range of possible activities in the CBD to include cafés, restaurants and wine bars. ■ Invest in theatres and other leisure facilities.	
5 Derelict buildings are left surrounding the CBD as older buildings are abandoned by their former occupants.	■ Reuse derelict land.	
6 There is traffic congestion and difficulty in parking in the CBD.	■ Improve access to the CBD by: **a** improving public transportation; **b** improving parking.	

The Oracle Centre lies on the outskirts of Reading. True or false? • Reading lies on the M40. True or false?

Why is the M4 corridor growing?

Reading's growth is partly the result of planning decisions made by the local council and private companies. However, it's also the result of Reading's location along a stretch of southern England known as the 'M4 corridor'.

Refer to pages 52-53 of the textbook as you work through this section.

Before you start the main revision activities, try this quick quiz:

1 Name two counties through which the M4 passes.
2 What is meant by the 'M4 corridor'?
3 Give three examples of hi-tech industries found along the 'corridor'.
4 Name the starting and finishing cities of the M4.
5 What is a footloose industry?

Revision activities

Read page 52 of the textbook and study Figure 1. Then close the book.

Figure 12

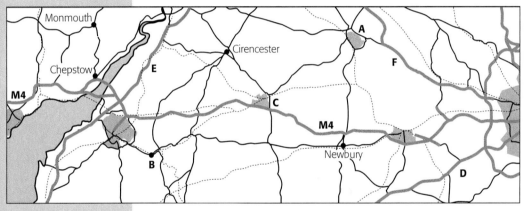

1 On Figure 12:
   a mark and name
      ▪ London, Reading, Bristol, and Cardiff
      ▪ The M25 and M1
      ▪ The Bristol Channel
   b name towns A, B and C
   c name motorways D, E and F.

Why is the M40 corridor so popular with 'new' industries?

This activity asks you to apply some of the ideas on pages 52-53 of the textbook. All of the companies are real and have large premises or headquarters along the M4 corridor.

Lower land prices, Heathrow Airport, good rail and road links, nearby universities, attractive countryside, and varied leisure facilities are some factors which explain the popularity of the M4 corridor to newer industries.

1 Consider Vodafone, a huge international telecommunications company with headquarters in Newbury (see Figure 12).
   a Say why each of the above factors could be important for Vodafone.
   b Now consider Microsoft (in Reading), Prudential (also in Reading) and Honda (located in Swindon). Repeat the above activity for each one.
2 How far do these companies have (a) similar, and (b) different needs?
3 Why could all these industries be described as 'footloose'?

Heathrow Airport is currently expanding by building which terminal: 2, 4, or 5? ● What impacts may the new terminal have on the region?

What words do I have to know?

There is no set list of words in the specification that you must know. However, examiners will know that you have probably used the set textbook, and will feel free to use some or all of the following words in the examinations:

accessibility	full-time	land use
agglomeration economies	function	leisure
bid-rent theory	host nation	manufacture
employment sectors	HQ	part-time
employment structure	industrial location	TNC
exploitation	informal	urban sprawl
footloose industry	infrastructure	urban-rural fringe
formal economy	land availability	working environment

The glossary in the student textbook will help you with the meanings of these words and phrases.

What other sources can help me?

Using the student textbook will give you enough material to take you to the highest grades. However, if you did not study Nike or Reading, here are some websites to give you background material on other case studies.

TNCs and employment campaigns
Nike is used by the textbook, which lists suitable websites (page 40). Almost all TNCs have their own websites, which are easy to locate, e.g. Unilever (http://www.unilever.com), Ford (http://www.ford.com), Microsoft, etc.
For workers' rights, see the International Labour Organisation:
http://www.ilo.org
Fair Trade in the UK is covered by the following websites:
http://www.fairtrade.org.uk/
http://www.fairtradefederation.com/
http://www.globalexchange.org/campaigns/

Reading
The website for the Oracle Centre is: http://www.theoracle.com/

Try these questions

1 Describe what a TNC is, and then use a named example to explain where it operates and the reasons why its headquarters and manufacturing sites are located where they are. (*9 marks*)
2 Describe how successful, or otherwise, a named campaign has proved to be against **either** child labour **or** unfair trade. (*6 marks*)
3 For a named city which you have studied, explain how both jobs and shoppers can be attracted back to the CBD. (*9 marks*)
4 Use a city which you have studied to explain the advantages of the urban-rural fringe for businesses and employees. (*9 marks*)

Coasts

What do I have to know?

The Coasts unit has two guiding questions for study:

3.1 How do physical processes help to create coastal management concerns?

3.2 How do human activities help to create coastal management concerns?

Each is split into key questions (a), (b), and (c) below, and these determine what you must know and understand.

3.1 How do physical processes help to create coastal management concerns?

Key questions	What you have to know and understand
a What physical processes operate at the coast?	■ **Know** the different marine processes of wave erosion, longshore drift, and deposition. ■ **Know** the different sub-aerial processes (those acting on the cliff face) of weathering and mass movement.
b What is the impact of these processes?	■ **Understand** how the processes above lead to cliff erosion and retreat. ■ **Understand** the threats caused by erosion to types of coastal land use, e.g. settlement and farmland.
c Why do physical processes need to be managed?	■ **Understand** how ideas such as cost-benefit can be used to assess the need for and type of management. ■ **Know and understand** the different hard and soft options for coastal management. ■ **Know and understand** how to assess the success and impact of management options, both in the area where these are built, and their effects elsewhere.

The specification states that you must have studied **one** stretch of coastline:

■ where physical processes have led to the problems mentioned; and

■ where management is trying to control those processes.

It must be a **stretch**; the example used in the textbook is Christchurch Bay.

3.2 How do human activities help to create coastal management concerns?

Key questions	What you have to know and understand
a Why are coasts such a magnet for development?	■ **Know** how the stretch of coast you have studied is used, e.g. for recreation, settlement, tourism, farming or industry, and why this stretch of coast has been a magnet for development.
b What impact do these activities have on the coast?	■ **Understand** how different uses and activities along the coast have had a variety of impacts on the coastal environment, e.g. pressure to clear forest, farming, visitor pressures, building houses or other tourist amenities, industries, pollution.
c Why is management of land uses needed at the coast?	■ **Know and understand** that there are differences of opinion about how the coast should be used, both now and in the future. ■ **Understand** *why* different users may have different views about how to manage the coast in future. ■ **Understand** whether these different activities or opinions can be reconciled for the future.

The specification states that you must have studied **one** stretch of coastline:

■ where human conflicts have led to the problems mentioned; and

■ where management tries to work out the best options for the future.

Again, it must be a stretch – not just an individual place. The example used in the textbook is the Daintree World Heritage Coast in northern Queensland, Australia. You may have studied a different area, which could even be the same area as that for question 3.1.

Christchurch Bay

The following material refers back to pages 54-65 in the textbook.

What is Christchurch Bay like?

Before you start the main revision activities, try this quick quiz:

1 In which two counties is Christchurch Bay?
2 What is the name of the spit at the eastern end of Christchurch Bay?
3 What is the name of the headland at the western end of Christchurch Bay?
3 Name three of the small towns along the coast of Christchurch Bay.
4 Name a holiday village which is under threat along Christchurch Bay.

Revision activities

These activities have been devised to help you to draw a sketch map, and also be able to remember the key features and processes which occur in Christchurch Bay.

1 Study the map of Christchurch Bay on page 54 of the textbook for 2 minutes. Try to remember where each place is. Then close the book.
2 Mark and name the following features on the Figure 1 map outline:

Barton-on-Sea	Milford-on-Sea	Hurst Castle Spit	Christchurch	Highcliffe	Hengistbury Head

Figure 1 Christchurch Bay

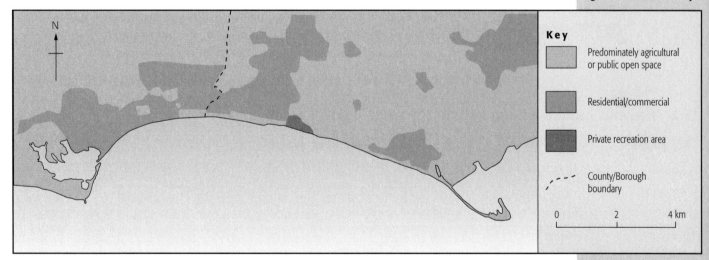

Key
Predominately agricultural or public open space

Residential/commercial

Private recreation area

County/Borough boundary

0   2   4 km

3 Now study the map of Christchurch Bay on page 56 of the textbook for 3 minutes. It shows the processes which affect Christchurch Bay and help to explain the erosion there. Close the book again.
4 Label the following processes on the map outline:

Winds (from which direction?)	Fetch (say what this means)	Which way waves most often break in Christchurch Bay
The effect Hengistbury Head has on parts of Christchurch Bay	How long the fetch is	Which part of the coast is most affected by storms and why

5 Now close this revision book and try to draw a labelled sketch map of Christchurch Bay, the places along the Bay, and the key processes which affect it.

Which of these numbers represents retired people as a percentage of the total population living in Barton-on-Sea – 25, 45, 65, 85?

Why is erosion affecting Christchurch Bay?

Turning words into diagrams

Sketch diagrams are helpful when explaining processes in physical geography. Use them whenever you can to explain processes in your answers. The following activities are designed to help you understand processes which:

- take place at, and erode, the cliff foot (page 56 of the textbook);
- take place on the cliff face – also known as 'sub-aerial processes' (page 57 of the textbook);
- occur along beaches – particularly 'longshore drift' (pages 60-61 of the textbook).

1 This activity will help you understand 'cliff-foot processes'. Read and study the diagrams on pages 56-57 of the textbook for 10 minutes. Then close the book and look at Figure 2 below, which shows two outline sketches of cliffs, (a) and (b).

Figure 2 Cliff foot processes

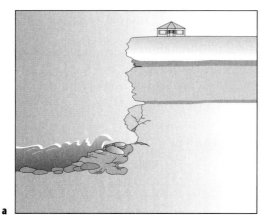
a

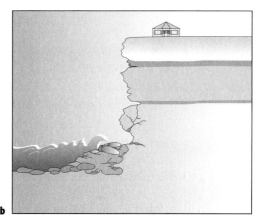
b

2 Add the following labels to the sketches in Figure 2. Use one sketch to explain the processes and the other to explain how the cliff collapses. The labels are all scrambled up, so you'll have to sort them out first!

cliff collapses	hydraulic pressure	wave retreats	air is trapped inside cracks
cliff is undercut	rocks thrown with waves against base of cliff	rock shatters	wave reaches base of cliff
an overhang develops	corrasion	explosion of air	

3 Next, draw **your own** sequence of sketches to show **cliff-face** processes. Use about half a page of notepaper for each one. Add the following labels which, again, have been scrambled up.

cliff cannot support its own weight	weathering	cliff becomes heavier	water soaks into cliff
movement of rocks	mass movement	cliff collapse	landslides
heavy rain soaks the cliff top	water soaks in along cracks and lines of weakness		
sub-aerial processes e.g. frost action or by solution			

4 Finally, draw a new series of sketches, each about half a page of notepaper, to explain:

a what is meant by 'longshore drift', and how it works;

b what groynes are and what they do;

c how a spit is formed.

Which is the odd one out and why – slumping, undercutting, abrasion, hydraulic pressure?

Protecting Christchurch Bay

Pages 58-59 in your textbook show several measures used to protect cliffs. Figure 3 shows the methods tried at Barton-on-Sea. Look for **revetments**, **cliff drains**, **planting shrubs** and **groynes**. Then try the following revision activities.

Revision activities

1   Using Figure 3, work out how each form of protection works. Make a large A4 copy of Figure 4 to complete with your answers.

Figure 3 Coastal protection – the 'Rolls-Royce' solution

Figure 4

Method	How each one helps to protect the cliff
revetments	
cliff drains	
planting shrubs	
groynes	

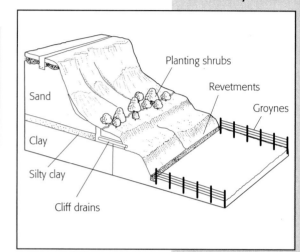

2   Now add **three** more methods used in Christchurch Bay to the table. Use pages 58-59 in the textbook to help you.

3   You should now have a full list, and you'll probably remember that each of these methods has its own advantages and disadvantages. Try Figure 5.

Figure 5

Cost-benefit analysis

The method used to assess whether or not a stretch of coast should be protected is known as 'cost-benefit analysis', where the costs of a project are weighed against its benefits. Figure 6 shows estimated costs and benefits of a new beach-nourishment programme to reduce erosion at Naish Farm.

Which methods ...
a cost a lot;
b are cheap;
c reflect wave energy without stopping it;
d absorb wave energy;
e work on the cliff face;
f work at the cliff foot;
g help to stop the cliff slumping;
h can actually increase erosion along the coast;
i make the cliff face more stable as a result of binding by roots;
j take water naturally away from the cliff;
k stop longshore drift?

Figure 6 Cost-benefit analysis

Costs of beach nourishment total £982,000			Benefits of beach nourishment total £1,610,000	
designing the work *£125 000*	the engineering work *£786 000*	annual checks, maintenance & compensation *£71 000*	saving property *£1 285 000*	saving local businesses *£325 000*
Costs of managed retreat			**Benefits of managed retreat**	
more/less	more/less	more/less	more/less	more/less

1   a   Using figure 6, describe how each cost and benefit is calculated for beach nourishment.
    b   Do costs outweigh benefits or vice versa? is the job worth doing?
    c   Now complete each cost of managed retreat, by comparing whether its costs and benefits would be 'more' or 'less'.

What is the difference between a sea wall and a gabion? • Why does 'managed retreat' NOT mean 'doing nothing'?

The Daintree

The Daintree is an ideal location to study places where human – rather than natural – pressures are affecting the coast. This revision study will help you to understand something about the place, the pressures it faces, and how its options for the future could either preserve it or develop it further.

The following material refers back to pages 66-77 in the *It's a World Thing* student textbook.

What's the Daintree like?

Before you start the main revision activities, try this quick quiz:

1. In which country is the Daintree? In which state?
2. Where's the nearest large town and international airport? How far away is it?
3. Name three of the small towns along the World Heritage Coast.
4. The Daintree rainforest measures a total length, as shown in Figure 1 on page 66, of which of the following distances? 50 km, 100 km, 150 km, or 200 km?
5. How long is The Great Barrier Reef? 16 km, 160 km, 1600 km, or 16000 km?
6. How many capes are there on the map on p. 66? What are their names?

Figure 7

Statement	True (tick) or False (with reasons)
Winter here is in June, July and August	
Winters are dry and sunny	
Most rain occurs in winter	
Summers are warmer than the UK	
60% of the annual total of rain falls in October, November and December	
Summers are wet, winters are dry	

Figure 8

	Rainforests in the Daintree	The Great Barrier Reef
What an environmentalist would believe is valuable about …		
They would think this because …		
If I was an environmentalist, the things I would most value about this are …		

Revision activities

1. Try to memorise the map on page 66 of the textbook, then try drawing an outline of the coast, marking on the tropical rainforest and the location of Daintree, Port Douglas, and Cairns.
2. Now study Figure 3 on page 66 of the textbook, which shows the climate of the Daintree. Tick which of the statements in Figure 7 are true, and correct those which are false.
3. Try this as a nine-mark, case-study answer. In it you need to:
   a describe the reasons for increasing numbers of tourists in Australia;
   b develop these reasons – with added detail;
   c use data to illustrate what you say.

This next activity is about understanding how and why people have different opinions about the Daintree. Spend 15 minutes reading pages 68-69 of the textbook. Then close the book and try question 4.

4. Make three copies of Figure 8. In each table, you need to explain how either (**a**) an environmentalist, (**b**) an economist or (**c**) a tourist would see the Daintree and the Great Barrier Reef.

Is the Daintree south or north of the Equator? • When is summer in Australia?

Developing an argument

This section is about helping you to develop an argument in your work. In this, you are going to learn how to work out whether further development would be good for the Daintree or not. Should it be allowed to develop, or should numbers of people living there be restricted to about 1200? Three stages are shown:

1   Identifying the main groups.
2   Completing a conflict matrix – assessing how much the groups agree with each other and why.
3   Deciding which are the strongest arguments and why.

Stage 1: Identifying the main groups

Read pages 70-77 in the textbook. Try to list in your mind who the key people involved in the decision to further develop the Daintree are.

Figure 9

Group	In favour of further development – yes or no?	Your reason(s) why
Port Douglas Shire Council		

1   On an A4 sheet of paper, start a copy of Figure 9. In it:
   a   say whether or not Port Douglas Shire Council would agree with further development in the Daintree;
   b   say why you think this.
2   Add to your table the following groups, then repeat the exercise for them.

Tourists	Environmental groups	Hotel or apartment owners in Port Douglas
Cattle farmers	The timber industry	Sheraton Hotel Group
Local estate agents	Local residents in the Daintree	Backpackers
Sugar cane farmers	Any other groups you can think of	

Stage 2: Completing a conflict matrix

Make a copy of the conflict matrix on page 13, and:
   a   add who you think are the six most important groups who would have an opinion about whether or not there should be further development into the Daintree;
   b   write their names in the left-hand column of the matrix, and again at the top of a column on the right;
   c   decide which groups agree with each other, and to what extent, using + or – symbols as shown in the key.

Stage 3: Which are the strongest arguments and why?

In this final stage, write out which argument you think is strongest – to develop the Daintree for economic growth, or to develop it sustainably by limiting the numbers of people living there. Time yourself, allowing no more than 10 minutes or 10 sentences. Remember once again to:
   a   describe which argument you think is strongest – to develop, or to limit the people living there;
   b   develop your reasons – with added detail;
   c   include data to illustrate what you say.

What is the link between deforestation in the Daintree and deterioration of this part of the Great Barrier Reef?

Which way should the Daintree develop?

Different people have different views about the Daintree. Some believe that economic development is the key to the future, whilst others believe that the World Heritage Coast should be preserved, and that development should be severely restricted. What do you think? The key to the future of the Daintree is 'sustainable development'. This means '*development which does not spoil or compromise quality of life for future generations by current practices.*'

Imagine two schemes, A and B:

Scheme A   involves bridging the Daintree River, extending electricity cables into the Daintree, and installing services which will encourage economic development.

Scheme B   involves limiting the population of the whole Daintree area to 1200, maintaining the present ferry, and limiting development to whatever can be accommodated using natural energy and water.

1   For this activity, read pages 74-75 in the textbook. Then complete Figure 10 as follows:

    a   Use the letter A to complete each of the 10 criteria below for Scheme A.

    b   Now use the letter B to complete each of the 10 criteria below for Scheme B.

    c   Add up a score for each development – it will be out of 20.

Figure 10

Positive	Very well +2	Fairly well +1	Average/no opinion	Fairly poor −1	Very poor −2	Negative
1 Uses or adapts existing facilities well						**1** Builds from scratch
2 Makes no impact on wildlife						**2** Makes a major impact on wildlife
3 Is environmentally friendly						**3** Is not environmentally friendly
4 Has a small adverse impact on residents						**4** Has a high adverse impact on residents
5 Vegetation is protected and encouraged						**5** Vegetation is destroyed
6 Involves using public transport						**6** Encourages motorists
7 Energy use is minimised or is all natural						**7** Energy use is wasteful and relies on finite resources
8 The wishes of local people are included						**8** The wishes of local people are ignored
9 The development would be affordable to all						**9** The development would be affordable only to the wealthy
10 Minimal pollution						**10** High pollution

2   Write bullet-point notes for a report which will outline what you believe to be the best way for the Daintree to develop in the next 20 years.

What have the following got to do with development in the Daintree and why – a ferry, electricity, tarmac?

What words do I have to know?

There is no set list of words in the specification that you must know. However, examiners will know that you have probably used the set textbook, and will feel free to use some or all of the following words in the examinations:

abrasion	corrasion	hard engineering	renewable energy	spit
beach nourishment	ecology	hydraulic pressure	revetments	strata
biodiversity	erosion	impermeable	salt marsh	sub-aerial processes
cliff face	fetch	longshore drift	Site of Special	sustainable
cliff foot	gabions	mass movement	Scientific Interest	weathering
conflict matrix	groynes	permeable	soft engineering,	World Heritage Site

The glossary in the student textbook will help you with the meanings of these words and phrases.

What other sources can help me?

Using the student textbook will give you enough material to take you to the highest grades. However, if you did not study Christchurch Bay, here are some websites to give you background material on other case studies.

Coasts with physical erosion problems

a The Holderness coast

http://www.hull.ac.uk/coastalobs/general/erosionandflooding/erosion.html
http://www.geography.learnontheinternet.co.uk/topics/holdernesscoast.html

b The North Norfolk coast

http://www.northnorfolk.org/coastal/default.html
http://www.geographypages.co.uk/ascoasts.htm - Although intended for students and teachers of AS Geography, this is useful for detailed background and some excellent pictures.

Coasts with problems caused by human development

a The Dorset coast, UK

http://www.dorsetaonb.org.uk/ This is the website for the Dorset Area of Outstanding Natural Beauty, with a substantial resource on coastal pressures caused by recreation and tourism.

b The Costa Del Sol, Spain

Channel 4's 'Geographical Eye over Europe', programme 7 'Stress on the Land' features the Almeira district of the Costa Del Sol in southern Spain.

Try these questions

1   Using a named coastal area which you have studied, describe how people have tried to manage problems caused by erosion, **and** how successful you think this has been. (*9 marks*)

2   Referring to examples of coastlines under pressure from development which you have studied, explain how and why conflicts have arisen between different users of the coast. (*9 marks*)

Hazards

What do I have to know?

The Hazards unit has two guiding questions for study:

3.3 How can tectonic movements create hazards?

3.4 What are the risks associated with flooding?

Each is split into key questions (a), (b) and (c) below, and these determine what you must know and understand.

3.3 How can tectonic movements create hazards?

Key questions	What you have to know and understand
a How do the processes operating at plate boundaries cause tectonic hazards?	■ **Know** that the earth's surface can be sub-divided into a number of plates. ■ **Know** that plate boundaries can be constructive, destructive or conservative. ■ **Know and understand** that movement at these boundaries can lead to volcanic eruptions and earthquakes.
b What are the effects of a tectonic hazard?	■ **Know and understand** the effects of either a volcanic eruption *or* an earthquake on the people living in the area.
c What management issues result from tectonic hazards?	■ **Know and understand** that various management strategies are used, both to plan for future events, and to cope with the aftermath.

The specification states that you must have studied **one** located tectonic hazard. It may be *either* an earthquake event *or* a volcanic eruption, and must be a clearly defined place, area, or region. It can be in either an MEDC or an LEDC and must show:

■ understanding of the physical processes that caused the event;

■ the effects on the physical environment and human inhabitants;

■ how management is trying to control the causes and effects.

3.4 What are the risks associated with flooding?

Key questions	What you have to know and understand
a How do physical processes lead to flooding, and how do human activities increase the risk?	■ **Know** the physical processes and human factors contributing to flooding. ■ **Understand** that the balance between physical and human factors may vary between one flood and another.
b How can the flood risk be managed?	■ **Know and understand** the different strategies used to manage flooding in MEDC and LEDC areas. ■ **Be able to compare** the strategies used in these two countries or regions.
c Why do people continue to live in areas at risk from flooding?	■ **Know and understand** the reasons why people continue to live in areas threatened by flooding.

The specification states that you must have studied **two** located flood events, of which:

■ one must be a *named and located* floodplain area in an MEDC; and

■ one must be a *named and located* floodplain area in an LEDC.

You need to know and understand the causes, effects and management strategies used for **both** of these case studies. It is important for you to be able to compare these events – it is not enough just to know about them individually.

How tectonic movements cause hazards

The following material refers to pages 78-89 in the *It's a World Thing* student textbook.

Before you start the main revision activities, try this quick quiz:

1 What scale is used to measure earthquakes?
2 Why do tectonic plates move?
3 What happens to rocks at the subduction zone?
4 Where do fold mountains occur?
5 Why do people continue to live close to some volcanoes?

Revision activities

1 Read pages 78-79 of the textbook, paying particular attention to the details about the earth's structure in Figures 4 and 5 and the text on page 79. Then have a go at the exercise below.

a In your notebooks describe what is happening at each of places A, B and C in Figure 1.

b Include details about the differences between the two types of crust shown.

Figure 1 Section through the earth

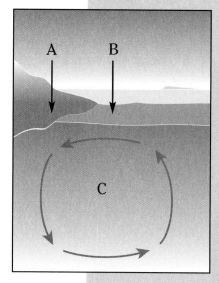

Figure 2

Tectonic true or false	
Say whether each of these statements is true or false. If it's true, move on to the next; if it's false, correct it in your notebooks.	
■ The outer layer of the earth is the crust.	True / False
■ The mantle is the coldest layer of the earth.	True / False
■ The crust is a continuous, undivided layer.	True / False
■ The crust is broken into plates which result from pressure caused by convection currents.	True / False
■ There are two types of earth crust.	True / False
■ Crust found on the sea bed is heavier than the crust that forms land masses.	True / False
■ The crust drifts around on the mantle, causing continents and oceans to move.	True / False

What words do I know?

See how well you know the following terms. Write each one down in your notebook with its definition next to it. Aim for the same level of detail as the example done for you.

Tectonics *The study of different sections of crust, and the landforms and hazard events which occur due to earth movements over time.*

Crust	Mantle	Plate	Magma	Lava
Seismic waves	Earthquake	Volcano	Fold mountain	Pyroclastic flow
Convection currents	Constructive margin	Destructive margin	Conservative margin	Collision margin
Mid-ocean ridge				

How much more serious is a Richter Scale 2 earthquake than a Richter Scale 1? • Constructive or destructive – what is the difference?

What processes occur at plate boundaries?

Before you start this activity, study Figures 1-4 on pages 80-81 of the textbook for 2 minutes. Then close the book.

Revision activities

1 **a** What is a 'plate boundary'?

    b Complete Figure 3 below to describe what happens at each of the four types of plate boundary.

Figure 3

Boundary type	Processes at work	Possible landforms & hazards	Example location
Constructive			Mid-Atlantic Ridge
Destructive			
	Two plates slide alongside each other. They do not move smoothly, and pressure builds up between the plates. This pressure is released very suddenly.		
		Fold mountains and earthquakes	

2 A good way of revising is to label blank diagrams.

    a Study Figures 1-4 on pages 80-81 of the textbook again. Then close the book.

    b Try labelling the blank version of Figure 1 below (our Figure 4).

    c Now try drawing and labelling the remaining three textbook figures.

Figure 5 Try this word search, which tests your knowledge of the effects of tectonic hazards. There are five hidden words for volcanos and five for earthquakes

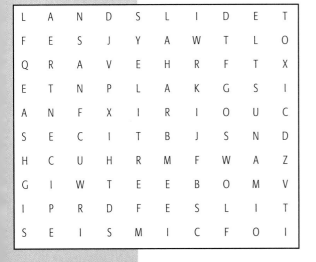

L	A	N	D	S	L	I	D	E	T
F	E	S	J	Y	A	W	T	L	O
Q	R	A	V	E	H	R	F	T	X
E	T	N	P	L	A	K	G	S	I
A	N	F	X	I	R	I	O	U	C
S	E	C	I	T	B	J	S	N	D
H	C	U	H	R	M	F	W	A	Z
G	I	W	T	E	E	B	O	M	V
I	P	R	D	F	E	S	L	I	T
S	E	I	S	M	I	C	F	O	I

Figure 4 Different kinds of plate boundaries

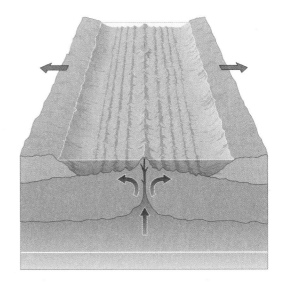

What is the name of the hills where the volcanic eruption took place in Montserrat? • What is the difference between magma and lava?

Can tectonic events be controlled?

Read pages 82-83 (Montserrat) or pages 86-87 (Turkey) of the textbook, then complete the following activities.

Revision activities

Using the heading words in the spider diagram, copy Figure 6 into your notebooks and complete it with detailed notes. It helps to explain the techniques used to control damage from tectonic hazards. One box has been filled in for you.

Figure 6 How can damage be controlled?

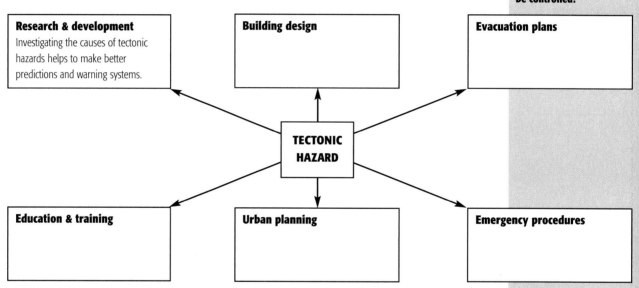

Research & development
Investigating the causes of tectonic hazards helps to make better predictions and warning systems.

Building design

Evacuation plans

TECTONIC HAZARD

Education & training

Urban planning

Emergency procedures

Developing your case-study knowledge

The largest proportion of marks in the section on Coasts and Hazards will be allocated to the case-study question. It usually carries 8 or 9 marks, so it is worth revision! For the exam, you will need to be able to remember many facts and figures about your chosen case study, **either** an earthquake **or** a volcanic eruption.

One method of helping you to remember details is to create a fact file. This gives details of the most important information. Study the example in Figure 7 and then complete a fact file for your tectonic case study. Make a blank copy of the Figure 7 grid to fill in with your own ideas. Include sections for economic and environmental impacts as well as social.

Figure 7

What?	An earthquake measuring 6.4 on the Richter scale
Where?	Maharashtra state in India (epicentre in town of Latur)
When?	1 October 1993 (4 am)
Why?	Movement of Indo-Australian plate towards the Eurasian plate, a destructive plate margin.
With what impacts? a) Physical	Seismic waves were recorded thousands of miles away in Delhi. The ground cracked and moved up to 2 metres apart.
b) Human	Social: 22 000 people were killed. Less than 20% of houses were left standing. Typhoid spread, due to the sewage-contaminated water. This fact file could also then include *economic* and *environmental* impacts.

Which years did the volcano on Montserrat erupt? • Which type of plate boundary is Montserrat on?

Flooding

The following material refers to pages 90-93 in the *It's a World Thing* student textbook.

Revision activities: What causes flooding?

First, you need to understand the physical processes at work when water travels from rain to a river. This involves you knowing key terms about the **hydrological cycle** and what they mean.

1   In Figure 8 below, some key terms and their definitions have been mixed up. Match each key term with its correct definition by writing the definition letter in the middle column.

Figure 8

Key terms	Letter	Definitions	Key terms	Letter	Definitions
Base flow		**A** The movement of water through plant cells into the atmosphere.	Precipitation		**I** Underground rock strata which are saturated and contain few or no air spaces.
Channel flow		**B** The movement of water confined within a river or stream.	Stem flow or drip		**J** The processes by which water reaches the soil or ground surface.
Evaporation		**C** The movement of water into the soil layers.	Through flow		**K** The processes by which water moves through the landscape.
Evapotranspiration		**D** The movement of water over the ground surface.	Transpiration		**L** Slow movement of water underground through saturated rock.
Hydrological cycle		**E** The combined processes by which water is lost by evaporation and transpiration.	Water table		**M** Underground layers of rock which contain air spaces and allow the passage of water.
Infiltration		**F** The upper level of saturated rock, which may move between seasons and years.	Zone of aeration		**N** Moisture in any form; liquid, gas or solid.
Interception zone		**G** Trees and other vegetation which prevent moisture from reaching the ground directly.	Zone of saturation		**O** The change of state from water as a liquid into water vapour, a gas.
Surface run-off		**H** The movement of water through the soil.			

2   Using some of the above key terms, complete the six blank boxes in Figure 9. Three terms have been given to you to use, but you have to work the rest out!

Infiltration	
Evaporation	Surface run-off

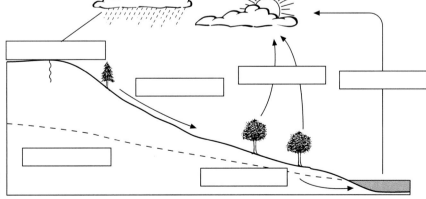

Figure 9 The hydrological cycle

Why does flooding often occur in springtime? ● What is the name of the graph which shows flood events?

3 The physical and human causes of flooding are described on pages 90-91 of the textbook. Read this and then complete the activity below.

a Study the images in Figure 10 and then complete the descriptions to explain the physical and human causes of flooding.

b Which of these elements are **human** and which **physical**? Write in the correct statement.

Figure 10 The physical and human causes of flooding

Deforestation: _____

_____

_____

_____

Physical or human?

Snowmelt: _____

_____

_____

_____

Physical or human?

Expanding urban areas: _____

_____

_____

_____

Physical or human?

Rainfall: _____

_____

_____

_____

Physical or human?

How flood risks can be measured

The most important method of recording flood events is by using a storm hydrograph (Figure 11). Hydrographs display information about the precipitation amounts and river discharge.

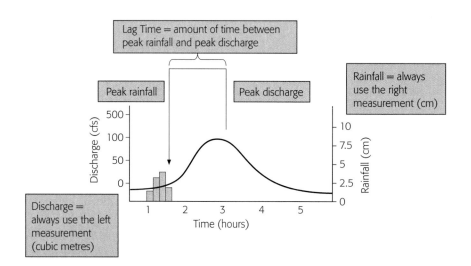

Lag Time = amount of time between peak rainfall and peak discharge

Peak rainfall

Peak discharge

Rainfall = always use the right measurement (cm)

Discharge = always use the left measurement (cubic metres)

Figure 11 A storm hydrograph

1 Study Figure 11 and answer the following questions:

a What was the peak rainfall?

b How long did the storm last?

c What was the peak discharge?

d What was the lag time?

e How long did it take the river to return to normal?

What natural water process is stopped when we build roads and houses? ● How do trees and plants help to slow down water flow?

Learning your case studies

For the exam, you need to know two case studies for this section; one from an MEDC, and one from an LEDC. The relevant textbook pages are:

- pages 92-95 for an MEDC flood, **or** a different study from your notes.
- pages 96-99 for an LEDC flood, **or** a different study from your notes.

Revision activities

1 Fact file. Copy Figure 12 into your notes and complete it for your chosen case studies.

2 Make an A4-sized copy of Figure 13 in your notes and fill it in. It should show the short-, medium-, and long-term impacts of your two floods. Try to show which impacts are:

- social (i.e. about people), e.g. numbers of deaths;
- economic – about costs, income, resources lost or wealth;
- environmental – which parts of the environment were altered.

Wherever you can, use data, e.g. numbers made homeless.

Figure 12

	MEDC	LEDC
Where?		
When?		
Why? (the causes of flood)		

Figure 13

	MEDC	LEDC
Short-term impacts (things that happened straight away or in the first few weeks)	Social Economic Environmental	Social Economic Environmental
Medium-term impacts (things that are caused by the flood but which take several weeks or months to emerge)	Social Economic Environmental	Social Economic Environmental
Long-term impacts (things that are caused by the flood but which may take place over several years	Social Economic Environmental	Social Economic Environmental

3 Now fill in the spaces in these summaries.

Figure 14

Tectonics:

The Earth consists of _____ layers; the crust, the mantle and the _____ . The crust is broken up into a series of tectonic _____ . There are four main plate _____ ; constructive, collision, conservation and _____ . It is at these plate boundaries that most _____ and _____ occur. The most famous area of tectonic activity is called _____ . Tectonic activity puts many _____ and environments in danger and it can take a long time for the communities to _____ . Techniques to control the effects of tectonic activity include _____ , _____ and _____ .

Flooding:

Rivers flood due to many human and _____ factors. Human factors include _____ and _____ . Physical factors include _____ and _____ .

Flood hydrographs show the relationship between _____ and discharge. There are a number of _____ used to control flooding. These include _____ , _____ and _____ . Flooding occurs in both _____ and LEDC countries, although LEDCs are much _____ prepared for the impacts of flooding.

What flood management technique starts with the letter L? • Is damage to the local economy a short- or long-term impact of flooding?

45

What words do I have to know?

There is no set list of words in the specification that you must know. However, examiners will know that you have probably used the set textbook, and will feel free to use some or all of the following words in the examinations:

TECTONICS		FLOODING	
crust	lahars	afforestation	interception
core	lava	alluvium	impermeable
conservative	magma	dams	lag time
constructive	mantle	deposition	levees
convection current	mid-ocean ridge	discharge	precipitation
destructive	plate	erosion	reservoirs
earthquake	pyroclastic flow	evacuation	run-off
epicentre	seismic wave	flood plain	straightening
focus	tectonics	hydrograph	saturation
fold mountain	volcano	infiltration	throughflow

The glossary in the student textbook will help you with the meanings of these words and phrases.

What other sources can help me?

The student textbook will give you enough material to take you to the highest grades. However, if you did not study the tectonic or flooding examples in the textbook, here are some websites to give you background material on other case studies.

Volcanoes

http://www.greenville.k12.oh.us/volcano/about.html
A basic guide to volcanoes with a quiz at the end to test your understanding.
http://vulcan.wr.usgs.gov/Outreach/AboutVolcanoes/
An excellent source of detailed information about volcanoes, including many case studies.

Earthquakes

http://science.howstuffworks.com/earthquake.htm
An informative guide about earthquake causes and effects.
http://news.bbc.co.uk/cbbcnews/hi/find_out/guides/tech/earthquakes
Good basic information about earthquakes.

Flooding

http://www.bbc.co.uk/schools/gcsebitesize/geography/water/floodsrev1.shtml
Clear and concise information about flooding, plus a test.
http://www.geography.learnontheinternet.co.uk/gcse/drainage.html
Flood information geared towards the GCSE examination.

Try these questions

1   Using either a named volcanic eruption or a named earthquake that you have studied, describe its impacts AND explain how people have tried to manage these. (*9 marks*)

2   Referring to examples you have studied of flooding, explain how and why the impacts of floods may differ between MEDCs and LEDCs. (*9 marks*)

Population dynamics

What do I need to know?

The Population dynamics unit has three guiding questions for study:

1.1 How is the population changing?
1.2 Why is the population changing?
1.3 What are the social and economic implications of population change?

Each is split into key questions (a) and (b) below, and these determine what you need to know and understand.

1.1 How is the population changing?

Key questions	What you have to know and understand
a How is the world's population growing?	■ **Know** what exponential growth is. ■ **Know** how and where the world's population has grown over the past 2000 years. ■ **Understand** how and why there are different predictions for the future growth of the world's population. ■ **Know and understand** how to calculate population growth rates. ■ **Know and understand** the difference between **actual** growth and **rates** of growth.
b Is population growth the same in all parts of the world?	■ **Know** the differences in growth rates between LEDCs and MEDCs. ■ **Know and recognise** differences between rapid increases, static and actual declines in population growth. ■ **Know** named examples of rapid increases, static and actual declines in population growth.

The specification states that case-study material is **not** required for this part of the course, but it does require you to know something about variations in population growth rates, sizes and characteristics of several countries for the examination. You should also be aware of the timescales involved, so that you know how growth rates can vary between static and exponential.

1.2 Why is the population changing?

Key questions	What you have to know and understand
a What factors contribute to natural changes in population size and structure?	■ **Know** what is meant by the population equation and population structure. ■ **Understand** how to calculate natural population growth rates. ■ **Know and understand** the role of birth and death rates and why these differ between countries in different states of development. ■ **Know and understand** that reasons for differences in birth and death rates may include health, education, religion, standard of living, and government attitudes. ■ **Know and understand** how to use population pyramids to show details of age and sex structure.
b How does migration contribute to these changes?	■ **Know** that migrations influence population change. ■ **Understand** how international migration (both emigration and immigration) influences a country's total population and structure. ■ **Know and understand** how to assess the impacts of migrations on population change.

You need a minimum of two contrasting countries to help you to illustrate reasons why birth and death rates and natural increase vary between countries at different states of development. It will help you to know the effects of migration in different countries, but the specification states that you will **not** be asked to refer to particular case-study material in the exam. The examples used in the textbook are Germany and Malawi.

1.3 What are the social and economic implications of population change?

Key questions	What you have to know and understand
a How do LEDCs cope with a growing number of young people?	■ **Know** that youthful populations are associated with many LEDCs. ■ **Know and understand** issues which influence family planning in LEDCs. ■ **Know and understand** the implications of youthful populations on dependency ratios and education. ■ **Understand** the roles of governments, individuals and NGOs in coping with growing numbers of young people. ■ **Understand** a range of strategies to cope with youthful populations.
b How do MEDCs deal with an ageing population?	■ **Know** that ageing populations are associated with many MEDCs. ■ **Know and understand** issues which influence family planning in MEDCs. ■ **Know and understand** the implications of ageing populations on dependency ratios, welfare and health provision. ■ **Understand** the roles of governments, individuals and NGOs in coping with growing numbers of elderly people. ■ **Understand** a range of strategies to cope with ageing populations.

This section concentrates on the implications of population change in both an MEDC and an LEDC. This time you may be asked to refer to case-study material in the exam. The textbook develops these issues through the study of Germany and Malawi. Don't be negative about populations; do look for any opportunities involved, as well as the more obvious challenges. For example, what are the advantages of having an ageing population?

To help you, different NGOs (Non-Government Organisations) are involved in population issues. Examples include Population Concern, Oxfam, Save the Children and Age Concern. NGOs often have their own websites and some issue CD-ROM materials, e.g. 'The population and development database' CD-ROM (Population Concern, 1998).

How is population changing?

The following material refers to pages 102-107 in the *It's a World Thing* student textbook.

Before you begin the main revision activities, try this quick quiz:
1 Which country has the fastest-growing population today?
2 How large was the world's population in 1950? 1975? 1993? 2000?
3 What does population-doubling time mean?
4 How long will it take for the world's population to double again?
5 Which country has the largest population today?

Revision activities

First, try this activity to test how well you know the basic terms.
1 Which one of the following explains the meaning of the term 'exponential growth' of the world's population?
   a When the population increases at an alarming rate.
   b When the population increases at a constant rate.
   c When the population increases by doubling itself.

While birth rates are falling in LEDCs, it is death rates that are rising in MEDCs. (TRUE/FALSE)

2 Which of the following mathematical sequences illustrates 'exponential growth'?
  a 1, 2, 3, 4, 5, 6…
  b 1, 2, 4, 8, 16…
  c 1, 4, 16, 64…
3 Draw a sketch graph to illustrate how the world's population total has increased since the first million was reached.

Figure 1 can be used to plot details of global population change. Read pages 103-107 of the textbook, then close the book and answer the questions below the map.

Figure 1 Global population change

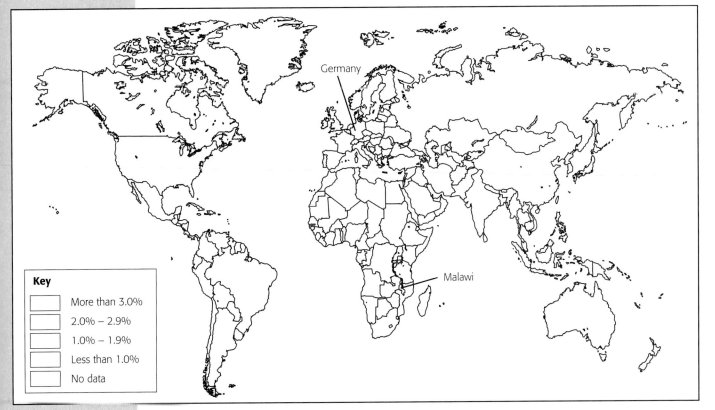

Key
More than 3.0%
2.0% – 2.9%
1.0% – 1.9%
Less than 1.0%
No data

4 After choosing four colours for the key, mark on Figure 1 four example countries for each colour/group.
5 Label on the map a line dividing the 'North' (richer) and 'South' (poorer) countries.
6 Define: (**a**) actual population growth, (**b**) growth rate.
7 Which parts of the world had the fastest growth rates in (**a**) 1950, (**b**) 2000?
8 Which countries are predicted to have the fastest growth rates in 2050?
9 What is expected to happen to the populations of many MEDCs in the first half of the twenty-first century?

Increased status of women added to the rate of children equals a strong control on birth rates. (TRUE/FALSE)

Why is population changing?

The following material refers to pages 108-117 in the *It's a World Thing* student textbook.

Understanding population change

You need to know and understand the following key terms and appreciate how they influence population change:

crude birth rate (CBR)	crude death rate (CDR)	infant mortality
life expectancy	fertility rate	natural growth rate

Revision activities

1 In Figure 2 below, match each term on the left with the most appropriate definition on the right. Write the correct letter in the middle column.

Figure 2

Term		Definition
Stable / replacement level		**A** If each couple fails to have at least two children, the next generation will be smaller.
Population decline		**B** If each couple has more than two children, the next generation will be bigger.
Population growth		**C** If each couple has two children, two new people will be left behind when the parents die, so the total population in the next generation will be the same.

2 Read page 109 in the textbook. Then study the attitudes or conditions for parents around the world, as listed in column 1 of Figure 3 below. In columns 2 and 3, suggest where these attitudes or conditions are likely to be found. (Column 4 is for a later exercise.)

Figure 3 It's an attitude thing!

Column 1 Attitudes or conditions	Column 2 MEDC or LEDC?	Column 3 Example country?	Column 4 Stage of DTM?
Modern birth-control methods are not widely available, are often expensive, and people have little understanding about such family-planning techniques.			
So many children die in infancy, that parents have big families in the hope that some will survive.			
Famine, unreliable food supplies, and poor diets influence decisions to have families.			
Big families are like insurance policies and provide children and grandchildren to look after the elderly.			
Improved infrastructure enables easier distribution of food and resources.			
Women are well educated and want to have careers, so they get married later.			
Material possessions mean more to me than children.			
Children are a blessing.			
Poor water supplies and limited hygiene.			
More food, better nutrition.			
There is improved healthcare, provision of vaccines and medicines.			
Educating my children is costly; they will work for the family.			
My virility gives me status!			
Family-planning advice is widely available.			
The infant mortality rate is falling – more of my children will survive into adulthood.			

Family size is as much a product of family planning as it is wealth. (TRUE/FALSE)

The demographic transition

1 Make an A4-size copy of Figure 4. On it, plot *lines* to show changes in birth rates, death rates and population size over time as a country passes through the demographic transition.

Figure 4 The demographic transition

High rates Low rates					
	Stage 1	**Stage 2**	**Stage 3**	**Stage 4**	**Stage 5**
Characteristics and conditions of society					

2 Use the bottom row of your copy to add descriptions of the conditions in countries at each stage of the theory.
3 Shade in the period of time when the population experiences 'transition'.
4 What happens to bring about 'transition': (**a**) in MEDCS? (**b**) in LEDCs?
5 Figure 5 below shows population pyramids associated with each stage of the theoretical Demographic Transition Model (DTM). Describe each pyramid in terms of (**a**) births, (**b**) deaths, (**c**) life expectancy, (**d**) infant mortality, (**e**) dependency ratios.

Figure 5 Five representative population pyramids

6 Match each pyramid in Figure 5 to the stage of the DTM model that it represents.
7 Now go back to Column 4 in Figure 3 and indicate which stage of the demographic transition model you associate with each attitude or condition.

Migrations

Read pages 114-117 in the textbook, which focus on migration issues in Malawi and Germany. Then make an A4-size copy of Figure 6 below, and complete it with points taken from the case studies in the textbook about these two countries.

Figure 6 Migration – Malawi and Germany

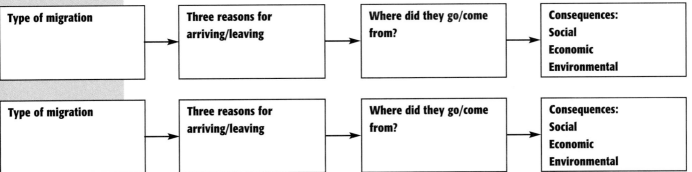

What families provide in rural areas of LEDCs, the state has to provide in many MEDCs. (TRUE/FALSE)

What are the impacts of population change?

This section deals with the consequences of population change in Malawi and Germany. It refers to pages 112-117 of the student textbook.

Revision activity

1   Study the population pyramids of Malawi (Figure 2 on page 112 of the textbook) and Germany (Figure 1 on page 116 of the textbook) and then complete Figure 7 below.
   a   Describe and explain the characteristics of each country's population.
   b   Consider the implications for each country.

Figure 7

MALAWI			GERMANY	
Reasons:	Description: High? Medium? Low?		Description: High? Medium? Low?	Reasons:
		Life expectancy		
		Death rate		
		Dependency ratio		
		Infant mortality		
		Birth rate		

IMPLICATIONS

		Demands on education		
		Housing provision		
		Jobs provision		
		Health-care provision		
		Welfare		
		Pensions		

2   Compare each country in terms of its GDP, literacy rate, types of jobs, percentage in school, and family size. You do not need actual data, just to know the differences.
3   What are the key issues for each country? Describe the living conditions and levels of development in each country.

If fertility rates fall, what will happen to the number of girls born? ● Having a high dependency ratio is as bad as having a high birth rate. (TRUE/FALSE)

Coping with change

For this, you will need to be aware of the ways in which governments of Malawi and Germany have tried to manage population change. Pages 119-123 of the textbook provide details of this. The following activity will help you to identify targets adopted by Malawi and Germany.

1 In your notebook, draw a table with two columns labelled: 'Malawi's young population' and 'Germany's ageing population'. Now list their characteristics.

2 Complete Figure 9 using pages 119 and 122-3 of the textbook to help you.

Figure 8

Read Figure 2 on page 119. Name 8 ways in which conditions in Malawi should improve.	Read pages 122-123. Name 8 needs of the elderly in Germany.
1	1
2	2
3	3
4	4
5	5
6	6
7	7
8	8

But will they work? How will they reach their targets?

Malawi	Positive aspects	Negative aspects	Germany	Positive aspects	Negative aspects
(a) Inviting TNCs in			(a) Voluntary work		
(b) Charities			(b) Charities		
(c) Self-help			(c) Government aid		
(d) Local rural industries			(d) Health care		
(e) Opportunities for girls			(e) Sheltered accommodation		
(f) Improved farming			(f) Subsidised services		
			(g) Pension funds		

3 Some countries have adopted an 'authoritarian attitude' to population control. **a** What does this mean? **b** Name an example. **c** How well did it work?

4 Others have opted for 'persuasion policies', e.g. 'family planning' and education programmes. **a** What does this mean? **b** Name an example. **c** How well did it work?

5 What are the social, economic, and environmental consequences of these policies?

One-child policies, mass sterilisation and population control are logical responses to overpopulation … aren't they?

What words do I have to know?

There is no set list of words in the specification that you must know. However, examiners will know that you have probably used the set textbook, and will feel free to use some or all of the following words in the examinations:

ageing population	dependents	life expectancy	population processes	stable population
asylum seekers	dependency ratio	malnutrition	population structure	standard of living
birth rate	economically active	migrant	pull factors	subsistence
cohort	population	migrate	push factors	
death rate	exponential	migration	quality of life	
demographic transition model	less developed	more developed	rate of natural increase	

The glossary in the student textbook can help you with the meanings of these words and phrases.

What other sources can help me?

Using the student textbook will give you enough material to take you to the highest grades. Here are websites for background or case-study material.

Population dynamics

a http://www.populationconcern.org.uk/ Now known as 'Interact Worldwide' for a full database and valuable case-study material, together with themed studies on population change.

b http://www.census.gov/ipc/www/idbpyr.html for population pyramids. http://geography.about.com/library/weekly/aa071497.htm for understanding population pyramids.

c http://www.os-connect.com/pop/ facts and figures on world population.

Why is population changing?

a http://axe.acadiau.ca/~043638z/one-child/thoughts.html China's one-child policy: what people think.

b http://www.populationconnection.org/kidfriendlycountries/Pages/countries/Malawi.htm

The implications of population change

a http://www.overpopulation.com/ for population and resource issues.

b http://www.bized.ac.uk/virtual/dc/index.htm for detailed case study on Zambia and everything to do with population and development.

c http://news.bbc.co.uk/1/hi/world/asia-pacific/906114.stm for China's ageing population.

Try these questions

1 Using examples of migrations you have studied:
  a describe the consequences of those migrations for both the source and host areas;
  b describe how local authorities have dealt with the consequences in both areas. (*9 marks*)

2 Name a country where the population structure has created a high number of dependents.
  a Describe the problems of a high dependency ratio in this country.
  b Explain how the government has dealt with these problems. (*9 marks*)

Population and resources

What do I need to know?

The Population and resources unit has three guiding questions for study:
1.4 What are resources?
1.5 What are the resource implications of population change?
1.6 How are energy resources being used?

The *It's a World Thing* student textbook takes these out of sequence – it considers energy issues (Question 1.6) before the implications of population change upon resources (Question 1.5). Therefore, the order of this revision book matches that of the student textbook.

1.4 What are resources?

Key questions	What you have to know and understand
a What are the differences between renewable and non-renewable resources?	■ **Know** the difference between renewable and non-renewable resources. ■ **Know and understand** the characteristics of some examples of renewable and non-renewable resources.
b What are the advantages and disadvantages of each?	■ **Know** that the use of resources has positive and negative impacts on the environment and the economy, and on people's standard of living. ■ **Know** what different resources are used for and understand why some resources are used instead of others. ■ **Understand** issues of exploitation, conservation and sustainability, with reference to renewable and non-renewable resources.

You need to know the characteristics of **some** examples of resources in each category, as well as definitions of the terms used in the content. Knowledge of case studies will **not** be required in the examination, but case studies used with Question 1.6 below could be introduced here.

1.5 What are the resource implications of population change?

Key questions	What you have to know and understand
a Will there be enough resources to support future generations?	■ **Know** that resource usage has increased as countries develop economically. ■ **Know** that population growth demands increased resource use. ■ **Know and understand** the Malthusian Theory and the link between population growth and resources.
b How certain can we be?	■ **Understand** and evaluate the Malthusian Theory. ■ **Understand** that the substitution and replacement of one resource by another, and strategies to manage resource stocks extend our ability to cope with the demands of the future.

The link between population and resources could be illustrated by a graph showing population growth against growth in resources. The evaluation could be based around a consideration of why Malthus's predictions have not come true yet, together with alternative theories, and how attitudes in the future (e.g. to recycling and sustainability) might have an effect.

1.6   How are energy resources being used?

Key questions	What you have to know and understand
a How can energy be produced?	■ **Know and understand** the characteristics of thermal energy production at a national scale in an MEDC. ■ **Know and understand** a small-scale renewable project in an LEDC.
b How sustainable are these energy supplies?	■ **Know and understand** how to assess and evaluate the sustainability of each energy supply.
c What impact does exploitation of these resources have on the environment?	■ **Understand** that energy usage has impacts on the environment, the economy and people's lives. ■ **Know and understand** positive and negative impacts at a variety of scales, from local to global – water and air pollution, greenhouse gases and global-warming debates.

The specification advises you to know in detail about:

■ **one** thermal energy source in an MEDC; and

■ **one** small-scale renewable project in an LEDC.

The MEDC study in the textbook considers nuclear power stations in France, and the LEDC study focuses on biogas digesters in India. You should make some links with the theme of sustainability here, as it gives you the chance to make links with Question 1.4 above.

Impacts range from the benefits of reduced deforestation (in the case of biogas) to local pollution and contribution to global warming (in relation to the thermal scheme).

What are resources?

Revision activity

1   Figure 1 shows six different resources being used. In column 1, annotate (or label) the items to show what types of resources they are, and in column 3 annotate their potential impacts on the environment.

Figure 2 Resources in action

Annotations: what is being used?	Image	Annotations: impacts on the environment?

MEDCs consume 81% of the world's resources, yet 81% of the world's population live in LEDCs. (TRUE/FALSE)

Resources: it's a growth thing!

As countries become more economically advanced, they discover and use a wider variety of resources. Each time a 'new resource' is used, it is said to have advantages over those used previously. But is this true?

Revision activities

Figure 2

- ■ Wood
- ■ Coal
- ■ Oil
- ■ Gas
- ■ Nuclear

1 For the listed energy resources in Figure 2:

    a explain why each was introduced; and

    b describe its advantages over the resource(s) that it replaced.

Example: *Steam ships replaced sailing ships because they were faster and less dependent on the wind.*

2 What other factors determine which resources we use? Make a copy of Figure 3 and complete it to show how each factor can affect whether or not we use certain resources. (*Hint – think about oil in the North Sea as an example.*)

Figure 3 Factors affecting resource use

Factor	How it affects the use of resources	Factor	How it affects the use of resources
a Cost of the resource		**g** Reliability	
b Accessibility		**h** Environmental laws	
c Availability		**i** Technology	
d Governments		**j** Quantity	
e Ownership		**k** Quality	
f Need		**l** Level of economic development	

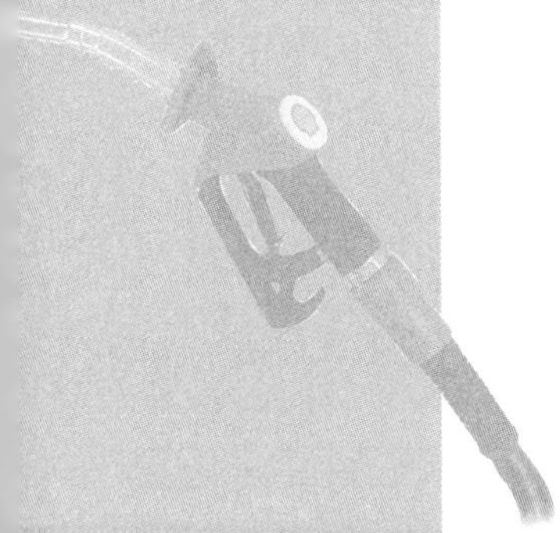

Even within countries, different resources are used for different things. However, the use of a resource can have positive and negative impacts on people, the environment and the economy. Read page 128 in the textbook and attempt these activities.

1 In Figure 4 below: (**a**) identify three different uses for coal; and (**b**) name three positive and three negative impacts of each use.

Figure 4 The impacts of different resources

Resource	Uses	Impact on people		Impact on the environment		Impact on the economy	
		positive	negative	positive	negative	positive	negative
Coal	1						
	2						
	3						

2 Now make your own copy of the table three more times, and repeat the exercise for (**a**) Wood, (**b**) Oil, and (**c**) Plant material.

3 Refer back to Figure 3, and explain how the factors listed have influenced ways in which one energy resource is used.

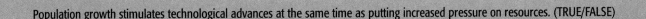
Population growth stimulates technological advances at the same time as putting increased pressure on resources. (TRUE/FALSE)

Population change & resources

Read pages 138-149 in the *It's a World Thing* student textbook. The next sequence of activities will test you on your understanding of that material.

Revision activities

1   Try to remember the percentages which show the distribution of wealth and resources across the world, between the rich 'north' (or MEDCs) and the poorer 'south' (or LEDCs). Then complete Figure 5. The important thing is not just to remember the correct figures, but what they actually mean.

MEDC (the 'north')	Percentage ...	LEDC (the 'south')
	of the world's population	
	of the world's industry	
	of the world's fossil fuels	
	of global emissions of carbon dioxide	
	of the world's cars	
	of the world's energy consumption	

Figure 5

2   Try this factfile quiz:
  a   How many children living in the 'south' would it take to consume the same amount of resources as one child in the 'north'?
  b   What percentage of the world is starving?
  c   How many people live in absolute poverty?
  d   What percentage of the world is overgrazed and poorly farmed?
  e   Which country consumes the most?

Population as a multiplier

Remember that pressure from population comes from two directions:
  ▧   firstly, an increase in population **total** puts pressure on resources – more people need more resources; and
  ▧   secondly, as countries **develop economically**, they tend to consume more resources, even without a population increase.

These two 'growth factors' mean that more and more resources will be required in future.

Theories about resource provision and consumption have been around for centuries. Two of the best known have totally opposite opinions! See if you can remember what **Thomas Malthus** and **Ester Boserup** predicted.

Revision activities

1   Who said that? Decide who said each speech bubble in Figure 6.
2   Who was right? Evidence points in both directions. Draw a table with two columns. On the left-hand side, list 5 things about the world **now** which support Malthus's view of world population; on the right, do the same for Boserup.

'Food supply grows arithmetically, whilst population grows geometrically.'

'If population, industry, pollution, and amount of food and resource use all increased, the world would suddenly face a disaster.'

'Technology will save the day...'

'Properly managed, the Earth could meet everyone's needs abundantly and indefinitely.'

Scientific advances ensure that more food becomes available to satisfy increased demand.'

'At the moment we are surely the brightest and brainiest of the Earth's working parts ... I trust us to have the will to maintain as best we can the life of the planet.'

'If the population continues to grow exponentially, then catastrophe will be inevitable... hunger, disease and famine will act as natural checks upon continued growth.'

Figure 6 Malthus versus Boserup: 'Nature versus Technology'

Sustainable futures offer everyone a future. (TRUE/FALSE)

The way ahead

Read pages 142-149 of the *It's a World Thing* student textbook before completing the next activities.

In your exam, aim for the highest level 3 responses. To understand these, consider the wider issues first. In understanding the relationship between resources and population consider the arguments for more sustainable futures (Figure 7).

Figure 7

1 What is meant by sustainability?	6 Can ideas suggested in MEDCs be easily transferred to LEDCs?	10 What are the most serious obstacles to change?
2 What can we do as individuals?		11 Whose responsibility is it to change?
3 What has been achieved already?	7 Are there too many people in the world? Or is it a matter of resource distribution?	
4 Reducing, recycling, repairing, re-using; are these possible?	8 Is it necessary to control population growth?	
5 Re-thinking our ways of life; is this possible?	9 What are the most serious outcomes if nothing changes?	

'Sustainable futures' are discussed in all areas of the specification, so, for the following activity, use **any** case-study material from any section. Sustainable cities (pages 22-29 of the textbook), agriculture (pages 198-221), and tourism (pages 238-245), offer examples.

Revision activities

1 Now make a larger copy of Figure 8 and use it to develop a level 3 response to the question: 'How can we achieve sustainability?'

Figure 8 Levels of response grid

How to achieve greater sustainability	**Level 1** Name an example and describe it	**Level 2** Explain what it is meant to achieve	Explain how the scheme works	**Level 3** Evaluate it Describe its good points	Evaluate it Describe its weak points
Reduce pollution					
Use brownfield sites					
Grow more food locally					
Resource substitution					
Waste less					
Use public transport					
Energy-efficient appliances					
Carbon tax					
Promote recycling					
Use renewable resources					

2 If the total population continues to grow, it becomes difficult to raise living standards, because there will be increased demand for all resources. Some countries, such as China, control numbers of people, as well as increasing food. How successful has China been?

A world without nuclear power is a world without light. (TRUE/FALSE) • Managing resources is OK if you've got them to manage! (TRUE/FALSE)

How are energy resources being used?

Revision activities: What is energy?

1   Draw a generalised scatter graph to show the relationship between energy consumption and GNP per capita.
    a   Is your trend a positive or negative correlation?
    b   Why is this the case?
    c   Can you think of any circumstances in which countries might not follow this trend as they develop?

2   Explain why 'types of energy used' changes as countries develop.

3   a   Compile a list of energy sources and reasons for their usage.
    b   Now rank your list, according to which, in your opinion, harms the environment the most.
    c   Why is this energy source still an important part of the energy mix for many countries?

The textbook uses two contrasting examples of energy use, France and India, on pages 130-137. Read these pages before attempting question 4 onwards.

4   Create an energy fact file for France and India using the questions below.

Figure 9 Energy fact file

France	Questions	India
	■ Identify the main sources of energy in each country; **and** ■ sketch two maps on a separate sheet to show the distribution of one type of energy in each country. Use labels to name areas where it is found.	
	■ Fill in the pie charts to show the percentage of energy consumed in each of these sectors: ■ Industrial ■ Transport ■ Residential ■ Commercial/Others	
Thermal = Hydro = Nuclear = Wind =	■ Where does the energy come from? State the percentage contributions for each country.	Thermal = Hydro = Nuclear = Wind =
	■ What are the main issues facing each country in their **future** energy needs? Clue 1: Demand Clue 2: Supply Clue 3: Environmental impacts	
	■ What are the future plans for each country's energy supplies?	

International agreements are essential if everyone is to enjoy the world's wealth. (TRUE/FALSE)

Energy production as a system

Revision activities

1   **a**   Find Figure 6 on page 131 of the textbook, which shows a system view of electricity production from a thermal power station. Study it for 3 minutes and make sure you are clear about inputs, processes and outputs. Now study Figure 6 on page 133, showing a diagram of a biogas plant. Close the textbook.

b   Draw your own systems diagram of biogas production. Colour code the inputs, processes and outputs carefully.

Inputs and outputs

1   Select which of the energy sources listed below have **positive** and **negative** environmental impacts and complete Figure 10.

coal	oil	gas	nuclear	wood	plant material & organic matter	water

Figure 10 Impacts of different energy sources

Energy sources with positive impacts	Social, economic and environmental impacts	Energy sources with negative impacts
	Air pollution (acid rain)	
	Water pollution	
	Global warming	
	Visual impacts	
	Employment	
	Standards of living	

2   Obtaining the inputs for each country's energy needs has an impact on the environment, the economy and people's lives. This activity uses the same 'Levels of response grid' as on page 59 to evaluate different energy sources. Copy and complete Figure 11 below to evaluate each of the energy sources shown.

Figure 11

Energy source	Level 1 Describe	Level 2 Explain what it is meant to achieve	Explain how it works	Level 3 Evaluate it Describe its good points	Evaluate it Describe its weak points
Coal					
Oil					
Natural gas					
Nuclear					
Wood					
Plant material					
Water					

Acid rain and the greenhouse effect are to sustainability as poverty and tradition/religion are to population policies. (TRUE/FALSE)

What words do I have to know?

There is no set list of words in the specification that you must know. However, examiners will know that you have probably used the set textbook, and will feel free to use some or all of the following words in the examinations:

Acid rain	environmental impact	Local Agenda 21	renewable energy	sustainable development
biodiversity	environmentally friendly	non-renewable	stewardship	
Brandt Report	global warming	quota	subsistence	
demand management	greenhouse gases	recycle	substitution	
ecology	GDP	renewable	sustainable	

The glossary in the student textbook will help you with the meanings of these words and phrases.

What other sources can help me?

Using the student textbook will give you enough material to take you to the highest grades. Here are some possible websites which will give you background or case-study material.

What are resources?

a http://www.wri.org/ The World Resources Institute provides detail on all resources.

b http://www.eco-pros.com/renewableresources.htm renewable/non-renewable resources in detail with interactive quiz.

What are the resource implications of population change?

a http://www.un.org/esa/sustdev/documents/agenda21/index.htm The Earth Summit, 1992.

b http://habitat.igc.org/agenda21/ The agreements from The Earth Summit.

c http://www.scream.co.uk/la21/ Local Agenda 21 programmes.

d http://www.rio-plus-10.org/ Earth Summit II, 2002.

How are energy resources being used?

a http://www.itdg.org/html/energy/expertise.htm Intermediate Technology works in LEDCs Solar Power/Micro-hydro/Biogas case studies.

b http://www.commondreams.org/headlines03/0813-05.htm Conflicts over French nuclear power.

c http://yosemite.epa.gov/oar/globalwarming.nsf/content/index.html An extensive site for links to global warming and the impacts of using non-renewable energy sources. Also the fun page for kids:
http://www.epa.gov/globalwarming/kids/

Try these questions

1 For either a thermal energy source in an MEDC, or a small-scale renewable project in an LEDC:
   a describe how it is contributing to the supply of energy;
   b explain what impact it is having on the environment;
   c say how far it is a sustainable development, giving reasons. (*9 marks*)

2 Population growth will continue to put pressure on the world's resources in MEDCs and LEDCs. Choose one MEDC or one LEDC and:
   a describe how population growth is placing pressure on resources;
   b explain how the use of its resources could be more sustainable in the future. (*9 marks*)

Water

What do I have to know?

The Water unit has three guiding questions for study:

4.1 What issues affect the supply of fresh water?

4.2 What happens when people try to improve their water supply?

4.3 How sustainable is our use of water?

The key questions below determine what you must know and understand.

4.1 What issues affect the supply of fresh water?

Key questions	What you have to know and understand
a Where do water supplies come from?	■ **Know** that rain is the primary source of fresh water, with fresh water stores, e.g. groundwater, rivers, ice.
b why do supplies vary?	■ **Understand** why patterns of rainfall vary globally – why there are variations in annual totals from place to place, distributions throughout the year, and reliability.
c What is water used for?	■ **Know and understand** how water is used for domestic, industrial, agricultural and leisure purposes. ■ **Know and understand** how and why consumption and use vary between MEDCs and LEDCs.

4.2 What happens when people try to improve their water supply?

Key questions	What you have to know and understand
a Why is the demand for water increasing?	■ **Know and understand** how the following have led to increased water demand and usage: ■ improved standards of living and hygiene; ■ increases in the world's population; and demand from agriculture, industrialisation and urbanisation.
b How can water supplies be increased?	■ **Know** the various methods of increasing water supply, including large-scale, river-management schemes.
c What are the impacts of river management on people and the environment?	■ **Know and understand** that physical and human factors influence the siting of large-scale, river-management schemes. ■ **Know and understand** the impacts of water-management schemes on the natural environment and human inhabitants, e.g. drowning of land, loss of settlements, loss of farmland and loss of biodiversity. ■ **Know and understand** why there are conflicts between the interest groups involved in water management.

For this question, the specification states that you must study **one** large, river-management scheme leading to increased water supply:

■ where physical processes have led to the water problems;

■ the management schemes that have been put in place;

■ the impacts that this has had on people and the environment.

4.3 How sustainable is our use of water?

Key questions	What you have to know and understand
a How are we spoiling our water supplies?	■ **Know** that industry, agriculture, transport and leisure uses of rivers and lakes can lead to their pollution. ■ **Understand** that there are strategies for dealing with this pollution.
b Can water supplies run out?	■ **Understand** that if the supply and demand for water get out of balance, it can lead to over-extraction and depletion of supplies.

You must have studied **one** case of pollution in a river or lake:

■ where physical and human causes have resulted in the pollution;

■ and the strategies being used to manage this pollution.

Issues affecting water supply

The following material refers to pages 150-155 in the student textbook.

Where fresh water supplies come from

Before you begin this section, it will help you to have revised Hazards and the general hydrological cycle, found on pages 39-46 of this book. You should make sure that you can complete the water cycle diagram on page 43.

Revision activities

Read pages 150-151 of the textbook, taking 5 minutes to look carefully at where water comes from in Figures 2-5. Close the book, and try the following.

1   Read the following statements and decide whether they are true or false. If they are false, explain why and correct them in your notebook.
   a   Over 85 % of the world's fresh water is stored in glaciers and ice caps.
   b   13.5 % of fresh water is in surface stores.
   c   People in arid regions rely mainly upon water from groundwater stores.
   d   Most global evaporation of water occurs over the oceans of the world.
   e   The global circulation of water is known as the water circle.
   f   Large artificial lakes which store water are called aquifers.
   g   Accessibility is very important in determining which source of fresh water is most appropriate.

Why water supplies vary

Read through pages 152–153 of the textbook and complete Figure 1.

Revision activity

1   Copy and complete the boxes around the map to describe:
   a   the amount of rainfall in each place (using words such as 'very wet', 'fairly dry', etc.;
   b   how seasonal the rainfall is in each place, i.e. does it all fall in one season or throughout the year? (One box has been done for you.)

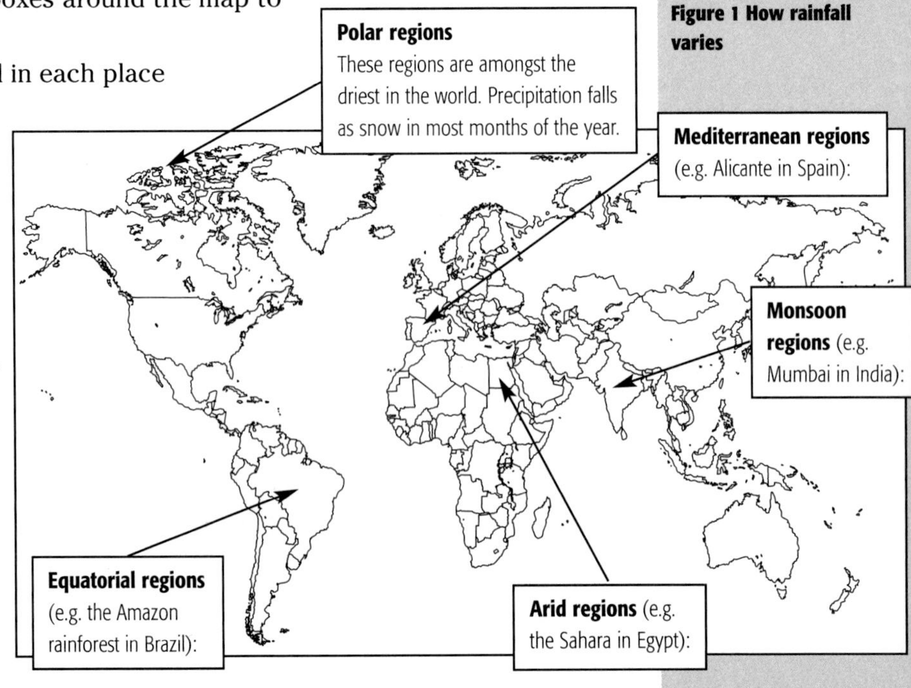

Polar regions
These regions are amongst the driest in the world. Precipitation falls as snow in most months of the year.

Figure 1 How rainfall varies

Mediterranean regions (e.g. Alicante in Spain):

Monsoon regions (e.g. Mumbai in India):

Equatorial regions (e.g. the Amazon rainforest in Brazil):

Arid regions (e.g. the Sahara in Egypt):

What is meant by water-rich? ● What is water stress?

How water supply varies

This page refers to pages 154-155 in the *It's a World Thing* student textbook. It helps you to understand how water usage may or may not match water availability.

Revision activities

Look at Figure 1 on page 154 of the textbook and try to memorise the names of the areas with the most and the least water. Spend 5 minutes and then close the book.

1   Make a list to show the countries with the highest (over 10 000 m³) and lowest (less than 1700 m³) amounts of fresh water per head.
2   How much of a MEDC / LEDC split is shown in your list?
3   Take 2 minutes to study Figures 4 and 5 on page 155 of the textbook, showing water resources in several countries. Then close the book. Fill in Figure 2 below. In it, state for each country:
    a   whether water available per capita is very high, high, fairly high, fairly low or low.
    b   whether water usage as a percentage of total available is very high, high, fairly high, fairly low or low.
    c   who the two biggest users of water are, e.g. farming, industry, etc.

Figure 2

Country	Water available per capita	Water usage as a percentage of total available	The two biggest users of water
Brazil			
Canada			
Egypt			
Israel			
Norway			
UK			

Figure 3 Water word search

F	T	S	Q	O	E	D	C	A	P
W	O	P	T	E	P	O	W	E	R
S	V	O	F	K	C	J	F	O	H
T	Q	G	D	X	I	R	E	Z	I
R	K	E	T	N	L	K	D	L	Y
E	H	E	J	P	B	T	B	A	U
S	F	I	N	D	U	S	T	R	Y
S	U	T	S	R	P	A	I	J	T
R	V	I	L	W	E	M	K	G	N
D	O	M	E	S	T	I	C	E	M

4   Using Figure 2, say what is meant by the term 'water stress'?
5   Using pages 154–155 of the textbook, try the word search in Figure 3, using clues a-f below to help you.
    a   This requires the highest proportion for its production.
    b   The UK uses 36% of its water for this.
    c   As a country develops, it requires more water for this.
    d   This is when a country requires more than 10% of its renewable water supply.
    e   As the population of a country increases it will require more water for _____ uses.
    f   The UK uses 51% of its water on this.

Figure 2 (photograph caption)

Which human activity uses most water globally? • Which sport uses the most water? (It's not swimming!)

Improving water supply

This page refers to pages 156-161 in the *It's a World Thing* student textbook. It helps you to understand how water usage may or may not match its availability.

Revision activities

MEDCs and LEDCs have different reasons why their demand for water is increasing, and have different methods to try to improve their access to water. This section needs knowledge of brief case studies. The textbook uses three examples of places, with three problems and three solutions from three of the world's rivers.

1   Read pages 156-161 in the textbook. Then complete Figure 4 below to link problems, solutions, and rivers.

Case studies	Problem	Solution	Which river?
The south-western USA (pages 160-161)		Damming schemes.	
Egypt (pages 156-157)	High per capita usage, caused by high living standards.		
Shanghai (pages 158-159)			The Huangpo River.

Figure 4

Increasing demand for water

↓

Problem:

Solution:

Details:

Example location:

Figure 5 Framework for studying water problems

2   Now take each study in turn and fill in a copy of Figure 5 for each one.
3   You need to be familiar with your chosen water-management case studies. To help you learn them, make an A4-sized copy of Figure 6 below and complete it for the three case studies.

Scheme outline	Egypt	Shanghai	South-western USA
What are the **physical** reasons for water problems?			
What are the **human** reasons for water problems?			
What impacts have solutions had upon the **physical** environment?			
What impacts have solutions had upon the **human** population of the area?			

Figure 6

4   Develop the following fact file about each case study:
- Where it is. Can you draw a sketch map?
- The past situation (e.g. did drought occur on a regular basis?).
- What techniques were used (e.g. was a dam and reservoir created?).
- The main purpose of the management (e.g. to provide irrigation for the local farms).
- Whether the scheme is/was considered an overall success or failure.
- The current situation of the area (e.g. does it have sufficient water?).

Why is demand for water increasing more rapidly in LEDC countries? • What is abstraction? • What's an aquifer?

Figure 7 Some problems caused by the Aswan Dam

Problems

1 Reduced silt
2 Increased erosion
3 Salination
4 Decline in water quality
5 Resettlement of people
6 Health hazards

Locations

- Offshore
- The delta
- Flood plain
- River banks
- Newly reclaimed farmland
- Lake Nasser

Figure 7 Some problems caused by the Aswan Dam

Figure 8 The effects of the Aswan Dam

Advantages of the Aswan Dam

This activity is designed to help you remember details about the Aswan Dam case study on pages 162-165 in the textbook. Read these pages for 20 minutes, focussing in particular on the maps on pages 164-165. Also look for **what** happened, as well as **where** it happened. Then close the book.

Revision activities

1 Using Figure 7, match the six problems with the locations (some problems occur in more than one location). Then label Figure 9 to match.

2 Using Figure 8, again work out which of the fifteen effects belong with which locations. Then label these on Figure 9 as well.

1 120 000 Nubians had to leave an area inhabited by them for generations.	**6** There has been job creation and economic expansion.	**12** Pollution from fertilisers is increased downstream.
2 Land has been reclaimed for farming.	**7** There is increased crop yields.	**13** Silt is no longer deposited, so artificial fertilisers must be used.
3 Bilharzia and malaria have increased.	**8** Erosion causes the riverbanks to collapse, losing valuable agricultural land.	**14** Subsidence is occurring and saltwater intrusion is a problem.
4 There is a high rate of evaporation.	**9** Fish stocks have increased.	**15** The shoreline is retreating by about 40 m per year.
5 There is a big increase in the land that can be farmed.	**10** Fish stocks have been reduced.	
	11 Floods no longer wash out salts from the soil.	

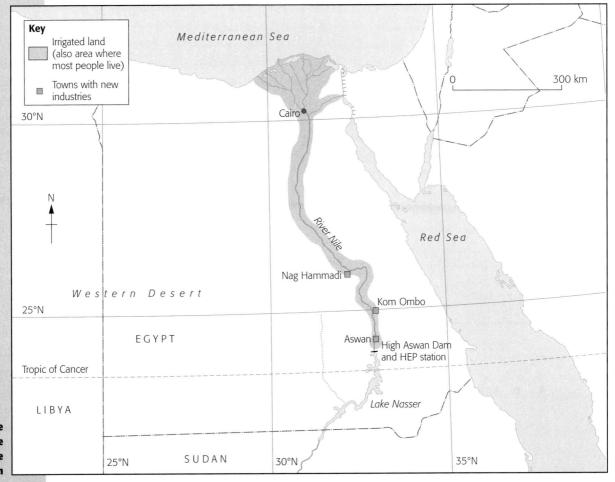

Key

Irrigated land (also area where most people live)

Towns with new industries

Figure 9 The Nile Valley and the effects of the Aswan Dam

What's the name of the lake created by the High Aswan Dam? • Which two colours make up the waters of the River Nile? Why?

The Aral Sea

There are many examples of water pollution. Some of them are short-term, such as the case study of the Danube in the textbook (pages 168-169). The Aral Sea, in central Asia, provides a longer-term case study. Read pages 170-171 about the Aral Sea disaster, then close the book and complete the following activities.

Revision activities

1 Which country is the Aral Sea mainly located in? Which country was the Aral Sea formally part of until 1991?

2 The Aral Sea is an 'inland drainage basin'. What does this term mean?

3 Figure 10 shows the outline of the Aral Sea in 1960.
- **a** Sketch the 1989 and 2000 levels of the Aral Sea on the map, in different shades of blue.
- **b** Shade areas of irrigated land in green.
- **c** Add the old fishing port of Muynak to the map.

Figure 10 The Aral Sea in 1960

As water levels have fallen, salt and dust are being blown *across the region* causing the loss of wetland ecosystems and valuable crops.

Cotton grown in the *Aral basin* requires high levels of irrigation and fertiliser to grow.

Water levels in the *Rivers Syr* and *Amu* have fallen due to irrigation demands; now little water reaches the Aral Sea.

Rice, another water-dependent crop, was also once grown in the Aral basin. This was required for local populations including *Muynak*.

The Soviet Union decided to grow more cotton in the *Aral basin*, thus expanding the farmed area and the amount of water used for irrigation.

The water in the *Aral Sea* has become increasingly saline and polluted, dramatically reducing numbers and types of fish and wildlife.

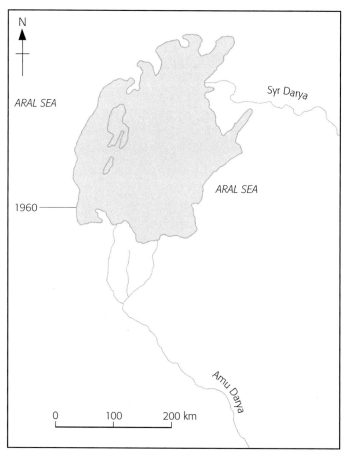

4
- **a** Draw arrows to link the above boxes to suitable areas of the map. (Use the words in *italics* as a guide.)
- **b** Shade in the boxes which explain **why** the disaster happened in red.
- **c** Shade in the boxes which describe **environmental impacts** in yellow.

Why does the Aral Sea look green from above? • What are the Syr and the Amu?

How sustainable is our use of water?

This page refers to pages 166-169 in the *It's a World Thing* textbook. Read them for 15 minutes before closing the textbook and trying the following activities.

Revision activities

Figure 11 Water crossword

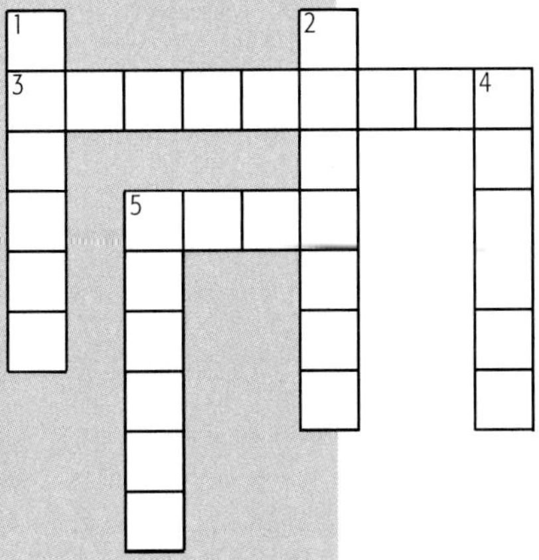

1   Complete the crossword puzzle (Figure 11).

Across:
3 Water must be used in a more _____ manner in order to meet the needs of the growing populations.
5 Seawater becomes useable by humans by removing what?

Down:
1 Increasing the supply of water by using it more sustainably is known as _____ management.
2 Importing foodstuffs which require a lot of water to grow is called _____ water.
4 This is a method of making householders use water more sensibly.
5 A country which lacks water is known as water- _____

2   The following exercise is about the River Danube disaster in 2000. Place the statements in Figure 12 into the correct order to show what happened; the first one has been done for you.

Figure 12

On 30 January 2000, cyanide leaked from a gold mine reservoir.	1
The aims included improving water quality and controlling hazards.	
Publicity included a free newsletter called 'Danube Watch'.	
The Danube River Protection Convention created an action plan.	
People's livelihoods were damaged and they lost income.	
Three weeks later, the cyanide reached the Danube.	
Water from the river used for irrigation affected the crops of the region.	
Fish stocks were poisoned in the Danube and its tributaries.	

If you have not studied the River Danube, you should create a similar exercise for your case study.

What lies ahead?

1   Read through pages 172–173 of the textbook, then close the book and for the countries or regions of Spain, China, Africa and the USA:
  a   identify the main issue facing each one;
  b   explain why each issue has arisen.
2   Would you say that water will be more of a problem for LEDCs than MEDCs in the future? Why?

What is meant by the term demand management? • What's virtual water

What words do I have to know?

There is no set list of words in the specification that you must know. However, examiners will know that you have probably used the set textbook, and will feel free to use some or all of the following words in the examinations:

aquifers	desalination	impermeable	run-off	water cycle
borehole	evaporation	infiltration	sedimentary rock	water scarcity
consumption	extraction	irrigation	sustainable	water stress
demand management	flood plain	precipitation	throughflow	water table
depletion	groundwater	recharge	virtual water	

The glossary in the student textbook can help you with the meanings of these words and phrases.

What other sources can help me?

Using the student textbook will give you enough material to take you to the highest grades. However, if you did not study the High Aswan Dam, here are some websites to give you background material on a variety of other case studies.

a   http://wwwga.usgs.gov/edu/index.html
U.S. Geological Survey's Water Education pages.

b   http://www.nws.noaa.gov/om/drought.htm
Causes and consequences of drought.

c   http://www.lalc.k12.ca.us/target/units/river/tour/index.html
A virtual tour of the Los Angeles River basin.

'Global Eye' magazine is on the web – http://www.globaleye.org.uk See Spring 2001 on 'Water'.

Aral Sea websites

http://nailaokda.8m.com/ A popular and detailed site about the Aral Sea.
http://visearth.ucsd.edu:16080/VisE_Int/aralsea/aral_map.html Interactive map of the Aral Sea.

Try these questions

Once you have completed the previous exercises on water supply, demand and management have a go at this 6-mark question. You will need to get used to giving longer, more detailed answers for both of the examination papers.

1   Using **ONE** named example, describe and explain the impacts of river management on people and the landscape.

Try comparing your answer with that of someone else.

Weather and climate

What do I have to know?

The Weather and climate unit has three guiding questions for study:

5.1 How can weather and climate be a resource?

5.2 How can people modify the weather?

5.3 How can climate change on a global scale?

Each is split into key questions (a), (b), and (c) below, and these determine what you must know and understand.

5.1 How can weather and climate be a resource?

Key questions	What you have to know and understand
a How do weather and climate attract tourists?	■ **Understand** that weather and climate can contribute to the economic success of an area. ■ **Know and understand** that weather and climate are resources which tourists use. ■ **Know and understand** that various aspects of weather and climate attract different user groups. ■ **Know and understand** the difference between weather and climate.
b How do weather and climate influence farming?	■ **Know** that weather and climate have a fundamental impact on farming success. ■ **Understand** that some parts of the world are better suited to certain farming types than others.
c How can weather and climate provide energy?	■ **Know and understand** that weather and climate are resources which can be tapped to provide sustainable sources of energy (e.g. hydropower and solar energy) and that some parts of the world are suited to these.

5.2 How can people modify the weather?

Key questions	What you have to know and understand
a How is the weather influenced deliberately?	■ **Understand** that some groups of people, e.g. farmers, deliberately modify weather to work to their advantage.
b What unintentional changes are taking place?	■ **Understand** that not all modifications of weather and climate are deliberate or desirable. ■ **Know and understand** that human activity can have negative effects (e.g. acid rain) and positive ones.

The specification states that you must have studied a named example of a place experiencing acid rain **or** an urban microclimate. One of these must be studied in detail, while an overview of the other is all that's needed.

5.3 How can climate change on a global scale?

Key questions	What you have to know and understand
a Is global warming really happening?	■ **Know and understand** what global warming is. ■ **Know** the causes of, and evidence for, global warming.
b What impact might global warming have?	■ **Know and understand** the possible impact of global warming on a region or country (LEDC or MEDC).
c Is the climate a sustainable resource?	■ **Know** that measures can be taken to reduce the risk of global warming. ■ **Know** that everyone, from individuals to countries, can take preventive measures. ■ **Understand** that prevention is better than cure. ■ **Understand** that not everyone is of the opinion that global warming is a significant threat.

You must have studied the possible impact of global warming on one region or country, which can be an LEDC (e.g. Bangladesh) or an MEDC (e.g. the UK).

Climate as a resource

Figure 1 shows climate data (temperature and rainfall) for two places, A and B. Both very different, they nonetheless encourage tourism and possess the climatic resources to do so. This activity will conclude by asking you where you think each place is – so think while you answer the questions!

Figure 1 Climate data for places A and B

Place A

	January	February	March	April	May	June	July	August	September	October	November	December
Temp (°C)	-6°	-4°	0°	3°	8°	13°	17°	16°	12°	6°	-1°	-6°
Rainfall (mm)	44	52	70	65	53	32	45	35	42	52	57	44

Place B

	January	February	March	April	May	June	July	August	September	October	November	December
Temp (°C)	19°	20°	22°	23°	26°	27°	28°	28°	28°	26°	23°	21°
Rainfall (mm)	75	69	71	99	161	254	170	175	210	164	116	67

Revision activities

1 Some of the climate data for places A and B has been plotted on to the graphs in Figure 2. Complete the graphs for July–December.
Remember that temperature is shown as a line, and rainfall as bars.

2 Are places A and B in the northern or southern hemisphere? Explain your answer.

3 **a** What and when is the *lowest* temperature for place A?
 b What and when is the *highest* temperature for place B?
 c Calculate the annual temperature range for each place, i.e. the highest temperature minus lowest temperature.

4 How do you think the two places might differ in terms of the activities they might offer to tourists? Give examples.

5 How and why might the two places differ in terms of winter and summer tourism and the crops grown there?

6 Suggest some possible locations for places A and B. Clue – they're both in the USA. Check if you're close by logging on to http://www.weather.com and inserting the name of each suggestion in the box at the top of the page. Then click on 'averages and records' towards the bottom of the page on your selected place. You need to use the 'mean' and 'average precipitation' columns. *The actual answers can be found at the bottom of page 78.*

Figure 2 Climate graphs

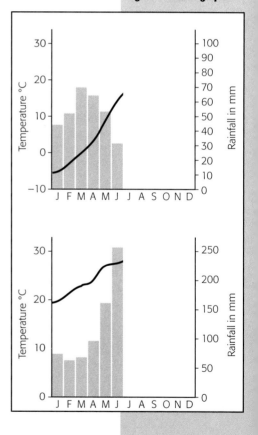

How are temperature and rainfall displayed on a climate graph? ● If temperature is recorded on a thermometer, how is rainfall data collected?

72

How do weather and climate provide energy?

This page refers to pages 178-179 of the *It's a World Thing* student textbook.

Revision activities: What kind of energy?

1   Read the information about hydro-electric and wind power and then complete the following summary table and complete the blank sections.

Figure 3

Energy Source	Climatic Requirements	Advantages	Disadvantages	Suitable locations
Hydro-electric power				**a** The mountainous regions of China **b** **c**
		Will help to reach the target levels of carbon emissions by 2010. It is free and will never run out!		

2   Dams for hydro-electricity provide problems as well as benefits. Write down five detailed bullet points to summarise why some people object to dams.

3   What objections are there to wind energy?

4   Which of these objections are (**a**) economic, or (**b**) environmental?

How do weather and climate influence farming?

Pages 180-181 in the textbook specify several ways in which farming is influenced by the weather. Read these pages carefully.

Revision activities

1   Study Figure 3 on page 180 of the textbook. For each of the ways in which farmers react to drought, give an example of a place you have studied or know of where this takes place.

2   Now study Figures 4 and 5 on page 181 for 3 minutes. Try to remember as much as possible and then close the book.

   a   Draw a spider diagram which shows the different factors that affect how and where crops can be grown.

   b   For each factor, write down an example next to it of either a type of farming or a particular crop that is affected by each factor.

What are tourist hot-spots? • Why is the tourist calendar said to have 'peak', 'shoulder' and 'low' seasons?

73

Urban hotspots

Areas of higher temperatures found in and around towns and cities, called urban heat islands or 'hotspots', are found in many major built-up areas.

How cities are different from rural areas

Study Figure 3 on page 185 of the textbook. Spend two minutes looking at it, then close your book.

Revision activities

1 Study Figure 4 below, which shows different weather elements. The right-hand column shows how cities differ from surrounding rural areas – but the data have been scrambled! Sort out which letter belongs with which element.

Weather element	Letter	Comparing cities with rural areas
Mean annual °C		**A** 10 % more
Winter mean °C		**B** 15-30 % less
Solar radiation, i.e. sunshine		**C** 16 % more, especially in summer
Precipitation amount		**D** 2–200 times greater
Thunderstorm frequency		**E** 25 % lower
Snow cover		**F** 3–7 times greater
Fogs		**G** 0.5-2 °C higher
Wind speeds, annual mean		**H** 4-5 days less
Calms		**I** 5-15 % more
Cloudiness		**J** 1–3 °C higher
Relative humidity		**K** 6 % lower
Particulates		**L** 60 % more, especially in winter
SO_2 CO (pollutants)		**M** Up to 20 % more frequent

Figure 4 Urban climates – they're different!

2 Figure 5 lists the ways in which various aspects of a city can modify its climate. The example used in the textbook is Atlanta in the south-eastern USA. Show how each aspect modifies the climate.

3 Many cities also tend to be wetter than surrounding rural areas. The nine statements in Figure 6 explain the process by which more rain falls over cities than the surrounding rural area – but they've been scrambled!

a Sort out which statement goes in which order.

b Draw a labelled diagram to explain how this rainfall forms, using the statements as labels.

Figure 5

- Tall buildings
- Central heating
- Street lighting
- Impermeable surfaces (like pavements, roads and car parks)
- Large car-parking area
- Traffic fumes
- Green spaces (like parks and gardens)

1 As rain droplets grow, they become heavy enough to fall as rain.
2 Condensation leads to cloud formation.
3 Dust forms nuclei around which water condenses.
4 Dust from the city is taken high into the atmosphere.
5 Higher temperatures warm the air.
6 Raindrops grow when small water droplets join up.
7 Rising air currents create unstable air.
8 The rough urban land surface slows the passage of weather systems.
9 Warm air rises because it's lighter.

Figure 6 How rain forms over cities

Name two countries where wind is a suitable energy source. • How is an ecosystem used to produce food?

Causes & effects of acid rain

This page refers to pages 186-89 of the *It's a World Thing* student textbook. You need to know how and why acid rain is formed, and some of its effects.

Revision activities

The best way to learn a process such as this is to (**a**) sequence it, and (**b**) visualise it by using a diagram. Study Figure 2 on page 186 of the textbook and then test yourself using the questions below.

1   Statements A-H in Figure 7 below describe the process of acid rain formation – rainwater reacting with gases which result from the burning of **fossil fuels** (e.g. coal and oil). Re-order the statements into the correct order.

Figure 7

> **A** Because of this, it's not always possible to identify the sources of acid rain.
> **B** These gases react with moisture in the upper atmosphere to form weak sulphuric and nitric acids.
> **C** The main sources of the pollutants which help to create acid rain are heavy industry and vehicle emissions.
> **D** Acid rain can be very harmful, damaging forests and crops, acidifying lakes, and increasing the chemical weathering of buildings and statues.
> **E** Burning fossil fuels releases sulphur dioxide and nitrogen oxides into the atmosphere.
> **F** The two most important pollutants which contribute to the formation of acid rain are nitrogen oxides and sulphur dioxide.
> **G** Pollutants can be transported hundreds of kilometres before being deposited on the ground.
> **H** Atmospheric pollution, therefore, becomes incorporated into the water cycle.

2   Add the numbers relating to labels 1-10 to the appropriate places on Figure 10 below.

Figure 8

1	Wet deposition – pollutants fall as precipitation up to 3000 km from the source.
2	Sulphur dioxide and nitrogen oxides are released into the atmosphere when fossil fuels are burnt by power stations, traffic, industry and for domestic use.
3	Farmland may be affected by the pollutants.
4	Gases are dispersed by the wind.
5	Lakes become acidic.
6	Acid snow – the pollutants are released when the snow melts.
7	Dry deposition – the pollutants fall as tiny dry particles up to 48 hours after emission and up to 240 km from the source.
8	Forests are damaged by acid rain.
9	Under the influence of sunlight, gases undergo a chemical change and react with water vapour.
10	Surface runoff is acidic.

What is a shadoof? • What does it do? • Where does it do it?

75

Global warming

This page refers to pages 190-193 of the *It's a World Thing* student textbook.

Before you start the main revision activities, try this quick quiz:

? 1 Which are the main greenhouse gases?
2 What's a technological fix?
3 Which city held the global conference on greenhouse gases in 1997?
4 Here's a quick one for you! Global warming – myth or reality?!

Revision activities

1 Read through the evidence for global warming in Figure 9. Tick the statements which are **true** and correct the statements which are **false** in your notebooks.

a Over the Earth's long history, the climate has fluctuated many times.	☐
b The most recent ice age was experienced in the eighteenth century.	☐
c Average global temperature has increased since 1860.	☐
d Some scientists state that there may actually be global cooling.	☐
e Methane is the most important contributing factor to global warming.	☐
f The burning of fossil fuels raises the levels of greenhouse gases.	☐

Figure 9

2 Study the ten statements about global warming in Figure 10. Decide whether you agree or disagree with each statement. Write down your evidence next to each one.

Figure 10

Statement	Agree or disagree?	Evidence
a "Global warming affects all countries – MEDCs and LEDCs."		
b "One way of reducing the effects of global warming is to lower the emissions of greenhouse gases."		
c "The main greenhouse gases are carbon dioxide, methane, nitrous oxide and oxygen."		
d "Global warming will eventually mean that areas of the UK, like Scotland, will receive less snow, threatening their tourist industry."		
e "The main culprit of global warming is the USA, which accounts for around 5 % of the world's population but around 25 % of global CO_2 emissions."		
f "Owners of vineyards in the UK might well welcome the effects of global warming."		
g "Since global warming is a world problem, it requires a world solution."		
h "The record temperatures experienced in the UK during summer 2003 are proof that global warming is a reality."		
i "It is the responsibility of individuals to reduce global warming, by turning off unnecessary lights and insulating houses efficiently."		
j "LEDCs, such as Bangladesh, are right to be annoyed with MEDCS. Since MEDCs created the problem, they should resolve it."		

What is the average temperature difference between rural and urban areas? • What is the difference between dry and wet deposition?

How will global warming affect the UK?

The specification states that you must have studied the possible impact of global warming on one region or country, which can be an LEDC (like Bangladesh or the Maldives) or an MEDC (like the UK). These activities look at the UK.

Revision activities

1 Read Figure 11, a newspaper article about the potential impacts of the enhanced greenhouse effect on the UK. Underline or highlight environmental impacts in one colour and economic impacts in another.

Figure 11

THE DAILY PLANET

The UK in 2050 – will we sink or swim?

Continued global warming may mean an additional two feet of water in the world's oceans. But how will this affect our little island?

The most obvious problem would be one of coastal flooding. This is where the sea level rises above the level of the coastline. This would result in the loss of valuable ecosystems such as the Norfolk Broads.

Another impact of a rise in sea level would be a reduction in productive farmland.

This means that there would be financial losses for both small businesses and the national economy.

In order to prevent coastal flooding, the government would need to put more sea defences along the affected coastlines, which is very expensive.

Although it sounds like the UK will be experiencing a washout, this is not the case. The southern areas of the UK will bask in Mediterranean summers, which will attract higher numbers of tourists.

This temperature increase would also benefit arable agriculture, allowing for higher yields of plant species previously intolerant to the UK climate. There would also be a longer growing season in the north of the UK.

On the other hand, some species of plants and animals would be forced out of their habitats by the rise in temperature, increased rainfall and new pests and diseases.

There are many potential impacts for the UK and whether you will sink or swim is more a question of what you do and where you live!

2 Study Figure 1 page 194 of the textbook for 2 minutes and then close the book. Try to list ten effects of global warming on the UK.

What can we do about global warming?

For this activity, read pages 194-195 of the textbook for 10 minutes, then close it.

Figure 12

Country	Rank order in total emissions/10	Rank order in emissions per person/10
Canada		
China		
Germany		
India		
Italy		
Japan		
Russia		
UK		
Ukraine		
USA		

1 Who's the culprit? Try this test of understanding. Place the ten countries in Figure 12 in order of (a) who produces the greatest total volume of emissions of greenhouse gases, and (b) who produces the greatest amount per person. Beware – the countries are in a different order from Figure 2 on page 195 of the textbook!

2 Five solutions have been suggested for global warming: technological fix, reduce global CO_2 emissions, carry on as we are, actions work, plant more trees. For each solution give an example and say how well it might solve the problems posed by global warming.

Name four possible gases which contribute to the enhanced greenhouse effect? • Which island country could disappear entirely by 2050?

What words do I have to know?

There is no set list of words in the specification that you must know. However, examiners will know that you have probably used the set textbook, and will feel free to use some or all of the following words and phrases in the examinations:

acid rain	ecosystem	hot-spots	irrigation	precipitation	temperature
climate	global warming	humidity	leaching	sun-lust tourism	urban heat island
desertification	greenhouse gases	hydro-electric power	microclimate,	sustainability	weather.

The glossary in the student textbook will help you with the meanings of these words and phrases.

What other sources can help me?

Using the textbook will give you enough material to take you to the highest grades. However, if you did not study the examples in the textbook, here are some websites to give you background material on other case studies.

General weather sites

a The UK Met Office - http://www.met-office.gov.uk/ - A good web page!

b For USA and global weather - http://www.weather.com/index.html

Urban hotspots and acid rain

a http://www.met-office.gov.uk/education/curriculum/leaflets/microclimates.html - Information about all microclimates, including urban heat islands. Atlanta is trying to counter negative impacts of higher temperatures in the Downtown area; log on to http://www.coolcommunities.org and click on some of the links.

b http://www.scool.co.uk/topic_quicklearn.asp?subject_id=17&Topic_ID=14&Quicklearn_ID=3&loc=ql - A basic guide to acid rain http://encarta.msn.com/encyclopedia_761578185/Acid_Rain.html - A detailed encyclopaedia article about the formation and effects of acid rain.

Global warming

a http://www.s-cool.co.uk/topic_quicklearn.asp?subject_id=20&Topic_ID=7&Quicklearn_ID=6&loc=ql - Information about climate and environmental problems.

b http://www.globalwarming.org/ - Up-to-date articles about global warming.

Try these questions

Once you have completed the previous exercises on weather and climate, have a go at these 6-mark questions. You will need to get used to giving longer, more detailed answers for both examination papers.

1 For either urban hotspots or acid rain, describe how it occurs and explain its effects on the environment. (*6 marks*)

2 Assess the likely effects of global warming on one named country that you have studied. (*6 marks*)

The answers to question 6 on page 72 are: Place A is Aspen, Colorado, in the Rocky Mountains, 250km south-west of Denver. Place B is Fort Lauderdale, Florida, north of Miami.

Farming

What do I have to know?

The Farming unit has three guiding questions for study:

6.1 What is the impact of modern farming methods?

6.2 What alternative farming methods could be used?

6.3 How can environments be damaged by farming mismanagement?

6.1 What is the impact of modern farming methods?

Key questions	What you have to know and understand
a Why are farming methods changing?	■ **Know and understand** that farming is changing and some ways in which it is changing (e.g. mechanisation, cost-cutting), and that these changes are linked to the increasing demand for food.
b How do modern farming methods modify the environment?	■ **Know and understand** some of the ways in which modern farming methods affect the environment (e.g. hedgerow removal, ploughing, burning, draining, irrigation, and the use of chemicals).

The specification states that you must have studied either **one** farming:

■ **system**, e.g. arable farming, dairy farming; **or**

■ **a region**, e.g. East Anglia, south-west England, Paris Basin.

This study must also be within the EU. The example used in the *It's a World Thing* student textbook is arable farming in East Anglia. The focus for the study must be the impact of changes in farm practices.

6.2 What alternative farming methods could be used?

Key questions	What you have to know and understand
a How may people and environments be affected by the development of genetically modified (GM) food and crops?	■ **Know** what GM technology involves, and how it differs from conventional farming. ■ **Understand** some of the implications of GM technology, e.g. altering the gene pool. ■ **Understand** why GM farming is controversial, e.g. the role of TNCs, the impact on organic farming.
b Is organic farming a viable alternative method?	■ **Know** what organic farming involves, and how it differs from conventional farming. ■ **Understand** some of the implications of organic farming, e.g. costs, impact on the environment. ■ **Know and understand** why organic farming is controversial, e.g. meeting market demands.

You need only have a general overview of GM and organic farming; no case studies are required. Focus on how individuals and groups feel.

6.3 How can environments be damaged by farming mismanagement?

Key questions	What you have to know and understand	
a How are fragile environments at risk from farming practices?	The specification states that you must study **either:** **a desertification** in an LEDC, in which you should **know and understand**: ■ how vegetation and soils in semi-arid areas are vulnerable to over-grazing and over-cultivation;	**or** **b deforestation** in an LEDC, in which you should **know and understand:** ■ how destruction of tropical rainforests can lead to soil erosion and flooding;
b What measures can be taken to ensure sustainable development in those environments?	■ how these can be improved, e.g. terracing, irrigation and water-conservation methods.	■ how this can be prevented or better managed, e.g. agro-forestry, afforestation.

The example used in the textbook is desertification in the Sahel in western Africa. You do not need specific country studies; a large area is enough.

Modern farming methods

The following material refers to pages 198-205 in the textbook.

The pressures on modern farming

Revision activities

Before you begin, read pages 198-201 of the textbook. Then study Figure 1 below. The following activities have been devised to help you to understand the factors which affect modern farming, and why it is changing so rapidly.

1   Make a large A4 copy of Figure 1. It is designed to show reasons why modern farming is under pressure.

2   Factor boxes 1-6 show three of the factors causing pressure on farmers nowadays. The two boxes marked 'A' help to explain why one of those factors has come about. Complete the diagram by:

   a   writing down more factors;

   b   explaining the reasons why each factor has come about.

   You can add more boxes than are shown, if you have more ideas.

3   Figure 2 below shows changes which have taken place on the farms themselves during the past 40 years or so, and how these changes have affected farms and rural areas. Copy and complete the table.

Figure 1 Factors affecting modern farming

- A Increase in number of animals, so price falls
- 1 Collapse in farm prices
- A People afraid of BSE, so demand falls
- 2 The EU
- 3 Supermarkets
- Factors affecting modern farming
- 4
- 5
- 6

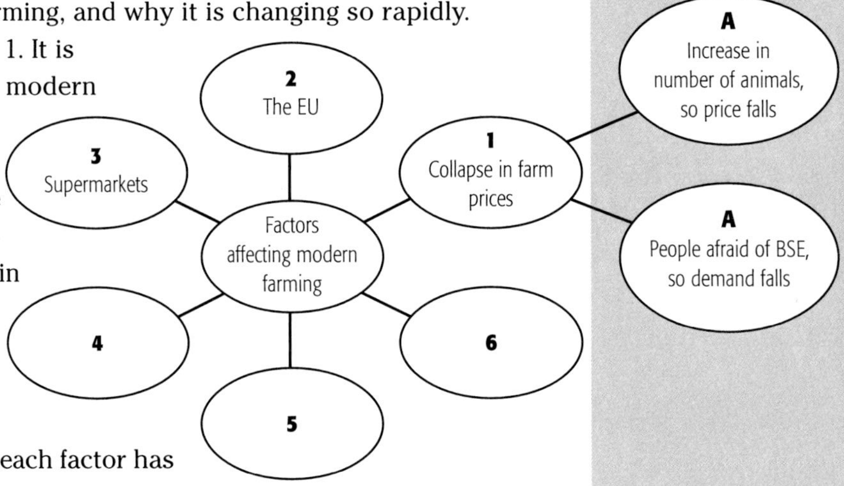

Figure 2

How farming methods used to be carried out	What changed?	Impact upon farms	Impact upon villages and the countryside
1 Cows were milked by hand	Mechanised, vacuum milking machines were introduced		
2			Fewer hedges are left
3	Tractors are more powerful		
4		Forced to produce less milk	
5	Supermarkets have gained a larger percentage of the UK's food market		
6		More humane methods of keeping animals are used	
7 Milk was sold directly to local dairies			Increased sales of farm products create jobs
8	Insurance companies bought up farms		

4   Have most changes been beneficial for the countryside or not?

Why is crop (or arable) farming based in the eastern UK? • Food miles – what are they?

Farming as an industry

This page helps you to use diagrams as part of your revision to aid your understanding about farming.

Turning words into diagrams

System diagrams are helpful in explaining processes in human geography. Systems consist of **inputs**, **stores** (within which processes occur), and **outputs**. Each input directly leads to a particular output.

Read and study pages 202-3 in the textbook for 15 minutes. In particular, look at Figure 3 on page 202. As you read page 203, try to remember the key features – not every figure! Now close the book, and try the following exercise, using Figure 3.

Figure 3 A system diagram for Lynford House arable farm

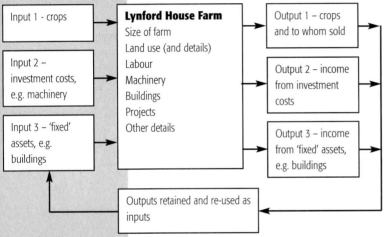

1 a Make a copy of Figure 3 on A4 paper.
  b Next, complete all the inputs as far as you can remember.
  c Add the labels about Lynford House Farm.
  d Now match the outputs to the inputs.
  e Are there any outputs which are retained as inputs? If so, complete the final part of the system diagram.
2 Why would this kind of farm be unlikely to survive with less than 750 acres?

Environmental impacts of modern farms

Farms use huge amounts of chemicals – fertilisers, chemical sprays to get rid of insects (pesticides) or weeds (herbicides). Many of these have severe impacts upon wildlife. One sequence can be seen in Figure 4 below.

Figure 4 The impacts of excessive use of nitrate fertilisers

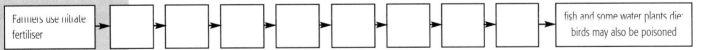

Figure 5

a Eventually, rainwater drains into streams and rivers.
b Fertilisers dissolve into the soil.
c Under stress from excess growth, algae produce toxins.
d Leaching occurs, where nitrates are washed down through the soil.
e Nitrates cause growth in algae and waterweeds.
f Toxins reduce the amount of oxygen in the water – a process known as eutrophication.
g Rainfall percolates through the soil.
h Nitrates enter rivers.

1 Figure 5 shows 8 statements about how nitrate fertilisers can lead to the deaths of water plants, fish and birds – but not in the correct order. Use these statements, correctly ordered, to complete the sequence on a larger copy of Figure 4.
2 Now complete similar sequences to show the sequence of events which lead to the impacts of hedgerow removal and soil erosion.

If seed is an input, what is the output? • 'Good for the economy, bad for the environment.' Is this the state of modern farming?

Organic farming

This page refers to pages 206-209 in the *It's a World Thing* student textbook.

Before you start the main activity, try this quick quiz:

1 How does an organic farm get to be 'organic'?
2 Can you use any fertiliser on organic farms?
3 How is weeding done on an organic farm?
4 How do you cross a strawberry with anti-freeze?
5 What's an 'agro-chemical'?
6 What is 'biotechnology'?

Organic farming is different from conventional farming. This exercise compares Aviaries Farm in Somerset (pages 206-209 in the textbook) with Lynford House Farm (pages 202-205).

Revision activities

1 Copy Figure 6 and use the copy to show how **inputs** at Aviaries Farm differ from those on Lynford House Farm. Also explain why these differences exist.
2 On a second copy of Figure 6, show how Aviaries Farm itself works differently from Lynford House Farm, and explain why. Use the system diagram, Figure 3 on page 81, to help you.
3 On a third copy of Figure 6, show how **outputs** at Aviaries Farm differ from those at Lynford House Farm. Explain why these differences exist.

Figure 6

Difference	Reason
a	
b	
c	
d	
e	

Are organic farms all they're cracked up to be?

There are different viewpoints about both organic and GM methods of feeding the world's people. Look at Figure 7 and fill in all the empty boxes with the opposing view.

Figure 7

Criticisms of organic farms	The alternative view
1 Food produced in this way is too expensive for ordinary people.	
2 You can't have efficient agriculture without pesticides and other spray chemicals.	
3 Too many rabbits and slugs!	
4	Organic farms have more buttercups and other wild flowers than conventional farms.
5 It takes so much longer to produce organic salmon or chicken without antibiotics – so they are more expensive.	

Why is dairy farming found in Somerset and the western UK? • What is an agri-business?

82

Genetically modified (GM) foods

The thing that makes revising a topic like GM foods difficult is that:

a there seem to be few 'facts' – the technology is still recent, and not a great deal is known (except what different people want us to know!);

b it is highly controversial and, therefore, it is difficult to separate 'fact' from 'opinion'. Governments, large multi-national companies, and pressure groups all have conflicting opinions.

The activities below have been written to help you to separate fact from opinion, to work out why different people have different opinions, and to help you clarify your own opinions on the issue.

Summary of the issues

- GM seeds have mostly been developed by American biotechnology companies, such as Monsanto and Avantis.
- The companies claim to provide drought-tolerant or insect-repellent seed, able to adapt to physical or environmental conditions across the world.
- The biggest issues focus on the legal conditions set by the biotechnology companies. Many companies are accused of writing exclusive rights to the seed or fertiliser into their farmers' contracts, which the farmers are forced to agree to.
- The UK government agreed to GM crop trials, as a result of which permission was given by DEFRA in 2004 to plant one variety of maize.
- Greenpeace and Friends of the Earth both fight against GM.

Revision activities

These activities are about helping you to work out what is fact and what is opinion in the GM debate. Read pages 210-213 of the textbook first.

1 Make an A4-size copy of Figure 8. It shows six statements about GM foods. If a statement is fact, tick the left-hand column **and** give the evidence. If it is opinion, do the same in the right-hand column. It may be both; so complete both columns!

Figure 7

Fact! Evidence?	Statement	Opinion! Evidence?
a	GM technology allows things that could never happen in nature.	
b	GM technology is just the same as farmers have been doing for centuries – mixing the best of one breed with another and improving yields.	
c	The poorer countries will lose out to the large American corporations.	
d	GM allows new 'golden rice' into the diet of people in LEDCs, thus preventing blindness.	
e	The large GM corporations sell GM seed to farmers only if they sign a contract not to keep seed from the harvest for planting next year.	
f	GM presents a real threat to organic farmers.	

2 Based upon these and other points on pages 212-213 of the textbook, draw and complete a spider diagram to show the points for and against GM.

3 Prepare a statement for a debate where you are asked to sum up your own views about GM foods. Use the following structure:

a What questions need answering?

b How far will they solve the world's food shortages?

c How far are there environmental threats resulting from GM?

d Will GM technology benefit LEDCs as much as MEDCs?

e What I think.

Life in the Sahel

The following material refers to pages 214-221 in the student textbook.
The focus for this study is the Sahel (Figure 9), an area which has suffered
drought for several decades. Try this quick quiz:

1 In which continent is the Sahel? The Sahel is part of which large desert?
2 Name three of the countries which are most affected.
3 What's the vicious circle of poverty?
4 What's the difference between a migrant and a nomad?
5 What does 'subsistence' mean?

Revision activities

1 Study the map of the Sahel (Figure 1 on page 216 of the textbook) for 2 minutes. Look at the names of the countries. Now read the section in the textbook about which countries are affected by the drought in the Sahel. Close the book.

   a Name the three countries shown 1-3 in Figure 9 below.

   b Say what effects the Sahel drought has had in each country.

   c Check the textbook to see if your answers are correct.

2 One of the major causes of poverty in the Sahel is deforestation. Mark the following statements in Figure 10 as follows:

   a With a 'C', those that show the causes of the deforestation problem.

   b With an 'E', those that show the effects of the problem.

3 People vary in their opinions about how far the damage in the Sahel is due to farming practices, population pressure or climate change.

   a Place these in order from 1 = 'most to blame' to 3 = 'least to blame'.

   b Justify your choice.

Figure 9 The Sahel region of Africa

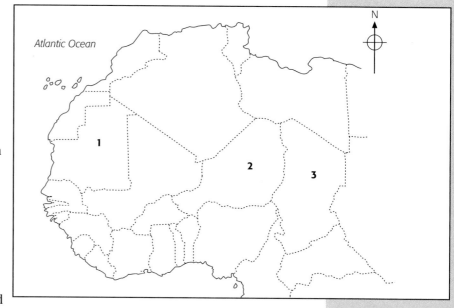

Figure 10 Causes and effects of deforestation

1 48 per cent of land cleared each year in Burkina Faso is to satisfy the charcoal demands of Ouagadougou, the capital.	
2 Even part-removal of wood can cause serious environmental effects. Pruning of branches may reduce a tree's capacity to grow; removing younger trees reduces the future potential of the forest.	
3 Fuelwood consumption in Mali represents an annual deforestation rate of nearly 400,000 hectares.	
4 In Mali, wood consumption is estimated at 5 million tons per year.	
5 In many LEDCs, demand for fuelwood is far greater than supply.	
6 In the Sahel, fuelwood consumption is between 30 to 200 per cent greater than the rate at which wood can be regrown.	
7 It destroys the soil's remaining protective cover and binding structure.	
8 It makes the forest open to wind and sun, erosion, less wildlife, and lowers biodiversity.	
9 It causes soil deterioration.	
10 It leads to the removal of nutrients which should return to the soil to maintain its fertility.	

What is the difference between the Sahel and the Sahara? • If deforestation is cutting down trees, what is the name for planting and growing them?

Giving the Sahel a sustainable future

Three projects are described on pages 218-219 of the textbook. Each is designed to improve the level of economic development in the Sahel. These projects work with assistance from other countries, known as aid.

Revision activities

Spend 20 minutes reading about the projects in the textbook, trying to focus on:

- what's happening;
- where it's happening;
- how it's happening;

- who it's intended to assist;
- how successful it's been so far.

Time yourself, then close the book.

Figure 11

Project	It is about ...	Key mnemonic
One	**M**ali, **I**rrigation, **S**eeds, **F**ertilisers, **Y**ields, **M**aize	**MISFYM** Or **M**y **i**nk **s**mells **f**unny, **m**um
Two	**S**enegal, **M**illet, **C**otton, **A**nimals, **D**itches, **Y**ields	**SMCADY** Or **S**ee **m**y **c**at **a**nd **d**og **y**elp

Figure 12 Projects in the Sahel

Describe its aims and methods	What are its advantages and disadvantages?	How successful do you think it has been?
Project 1		
Project 2		
Project 3		

Try the approach in Figure 11 to help you remember details – it uses a technique called 'mnemonics'. It is helpful where you have to remember several details in order to construct an account. It uses the initial letters of key terms to trigger your memory (to help you remember sequences of key terms). You can surely think up better and more memerable ones, but it does work as a technique.

1 Make an A4-size copy of Figure 12, trying to remember each of the schemes, using mnemonics or any other trick you use.

a 'When I send my child away for six months to learn how to tend the cows, he will return with useful knowledge that can help our family survive, and a little cow as his wage for the assistance he has given. With what will my child return if I send him away to school for six years?'

b 'We have cut down all our trees and, as a result, the wind makes us suffer because it erodes the soil.'

c 'We remember when, to find firewood, we only had to look behind our houses; today we have to walk up to 8 or 9 kilometres.'

Improving life for the Sahel's poorest

Now read pages 220-221 in the textbook, which are about projects that involve local people working together. These projects are advantageous, not just because they are cheap, but because projects which use local initiative and the skills of the people have been proven to be extremely effective.

Revision activities

1 Read quotes (**a**), (**b**), and (**c**) from people in the village of Siguin Voussé, about which pages 220-221 in the textbook have been written. Write a reply to each person quoted to show how aid projects of the kind described on pages 220-221 can help them.
2 Show how far each of the three projects – loans, diguettes, and education – fits the criteria for sustainable development on page 221 of the textbook.

What is the link between a diguette and a school? • What is a hybrid seed?

What words do I have to know?

There is no set list of words in the specification that you must know. However, examiners will know that you have probably used the set textbook, and will feel free to use some or all of the following words in the exam:

agri-business	borehole	genetically modified	irrigation	organic farming	soil erosion
agro-chemical	deforestation	habitat	malnutrition	pesticide	subsistence
arable	desertification	herbicide	mechanisation	quota	topsoil
artificial fertiliser	diguette	hybrid	migrate	Sahel	
bio-diversity	farming system	intensive farming	nomadic	set-aside	

The glossary in the student textbook will help you with the meanings of these words and phrases.

What other sources can help me?

Using the student textbook will give you enough material to take you to the highest grades. However, here are some websites to give you background material on other case studies.

General farming websites

For farming in the UK, the NFU website http://www.nfu.org.uk is very detailed. It is an excellent website.

The UK government view on farming issues can be found on DEFRA's web page – http://www.defra.gov.uk

GM, biotechnology, and organic farming

Look at different arguments presented by

a TNCs, e.g. Monsanto – http://www.monsanto.com

b Environmental pressure groups, e.g.
Friends of the Earth – http://www.foe.org.uk
Greenpeace – http://www.greenpeace.org

Desertification in LEDCs

BBC 'World 2000' video series

Oxfam's website – http://www.oxfam.org as well as websites for Action Aid (http://www.actionaid.org.uk) or the United Nations Development Programme – http://www.undp.org - more for adults or very bright GCSE students.

Deforestation in LEDCs

Global Eye magazine is on the web – http://www.globaleye.org.uk See Summer 2000 on 'Sustainable Development', focusing on agro-forestry in Cameroon.

Try these questions

1. Describe and explain how changes in farming have led to changes in (**a**) villages and farms, (**b**) rural environments. (*6 marks*)

2. For either GM or organic methods of farming, describe (**a**) how this method differs from conventional farming, and (**b**) why people have differing views about its effectiveness as a means of feeding the world. (*6 marks*)

3. Name an area which you have studied that is suffering from environmental damage. For this area, describe the causes of this damage, and the effects it has had on people and lifestyles there. (*6 marks*)

Recreation and tourism

What do I have to know?

This unit has three guiding questions for study:

7.1 Why is the countryside being used more for recreation?

7.2 What are the opportunities and challenges that visitors bring to the countryside?

7.3 What can be done to manage the countryside sustainably?

Each is split into the key questions shown below and these determine what you need to know and understand.

7.1 Why is the countryside being used more for recreation?

Key questions	What you have to know and understand
a What trends in MEDCs are encouraging more people to visit the countryside?	■ **Know and understand** why people are visiting the countryside, such as greater wealth, increased mobility and leisure time, and changes in lifestyles.
b How do contrasting rural landscapes provide different opportunities for recreation?	*In relation to one named national park in the EU:* ■ **Know** the features there that attract people. ■ **Know and understand** how the attractions there may result from rock type, relief and vegetation.
c How does the accessibility of a rural area affect the volume of visitors it receives?	*In relation to one named national park in the EU:* ■ **Know** the transport networks serving it and the nearby urban areas from which its visitors come. ■ **Know and understand** the importance of these networks in bringing visitors, and why numbers of visitors to some parks are greater than to others.

7.2 What are the opportunities and challenges that visitors bring to the countryside?

Key questions	What you have to know and understand
a How are residents of honey-pots affected by visitors?	*In relation to one named national park in the EU:* ■ **Know and understand** that visitors may bring economic advantages to an area, but that there may be economic problems (e.g. seasonality of work, high house prices).
b How are the environment and wildlife endangered by overuse?	■ **Know and understand** how uses by visitors may result in environmental issues such as air, noise and visual pollution, footpath erosion, vandalism and the destruction of habitats.

7.3 What can be done to manage the countryside sustainably?

Key questions	What you have to know and understand
a How can the countryside be protected from conflicting pressures?	■ **Understand** the conflicts of use in national parks and the role of planning and management in protecting the landscape.
b How can eco-tourism help more sustainable development?	■ **Know and understand** the issues involved, such as the impacts on local communities, conservation of the environment and wildlife, and sustainability.

Although there are general trends which you should understand, the majority of what you study will come from:

■ changing tourism in one named national park in the EU;

■ eco-tourism in an LEDC.

The examples in the *It's a World Thing* student textbook are the Lake District and the CAMPFIRE Project in Zimbabwe.

Changing patterns of tourism

This page refers to pages 222-225 in the *It's a World Thing* student textbook.

Changing holiday patterns

The following questions test your abilities in using skills to interpret information; something that examiners will also do.

Revision activities

1 Study Figure 1 and answer the following questions:
   a What was the value of employment in tourism in 1970?
   b How much had it increased to by 1995?
   c What sorts of reasons may have led to this increase in employment in tourism?
   d Suggest examples of the kinds of jobs that have become more important since 1960.
   e If this rise continued, estimate the value of employment in tourism to the UK economy in (i) 2000, (ii) 2005.

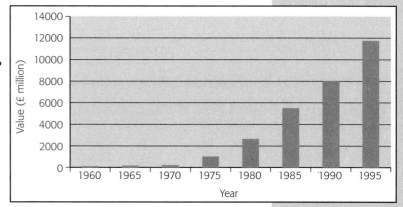

Figure 1 Employment in tourism by value (£ million)

2 Figure 2 shows figures for tourist trips from 1995.
   a What is the rise in tourist trips between 1995 and 2002 for the UK as a whole?
   b Which of the three constituent countries of the UK has the largest number of visitors? Why is this so?
   c Suggest possible reasons why tourism fell between 2000 and 2001. There are several possibilities.
   d Suggest possible reasons why English tourism grew during the period shown, but Welsh, Scottish and Northern Irish tourism did not.

Figure 2 Millions of trips taken in the UK, 1995-2002

Year	UK	England	Scotland	Wales	Northern Ireland
1995	147.79	114.05	17.53	12.79	3.42
1996	154.22	117.33	19.63	13.60	3.66
1997	162.23	125.55	21.19	12.25	3.24
1998	148.82	115.43	18.91	12.27	2.21
1999	173.10	137.71	18.53	13.37	3.49
2000	175.37	140.43	18.96	13.35	2.63
2001	163.10	131.90	17.50	11.60	2.1
2002	167.34	134.90	18.53	11.95	1.96

Source: Domestic Tourism Trends, 1995-2002 (Figures are for million trips taken.)

3 Figure 3 shows destinations for tourists leaving the UK for overseas trips.
   a What percentage of UK tourists holiday within the European Union?
   b What reasons are there for UK citizens to holiday within the EU?
   c Which countries do you think are the most popular? Explain your selections.
   d What changes to the tourism industry in recent years have made foreign travel easier?
4 Use the following factors to write sentences explaining why many people take more holidays than ever, both within the UK and overseas: amount of leisure time, income, mobility, cost of travel.

Figure 3 Destinations for tourists leaving the UK for overseas trips

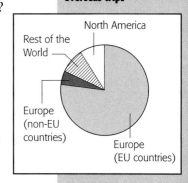

What recent events may lead to a fall in visitors to the USA? • Is it cheaper to travel abroad during term-time or in the school holidays?

Protecting the countryside

This page refers to pages 226-229 in the *It's a World Thing* student textbook. It focuses on the case study needed for a study of an EU National Park, and follows the Lake District National Park case study in the textbook.

Quick quiz – fact file!

Before you start the main revision activities, try this quick quiz. It will help to build up a fact file on your National Park case study. The questions are about the Lake District, so you should change them if you have studied another National Park.

1 In which county is the Lake District National Park?
2 What are its key rock types?
3 What is the landscape like?
4 Name the main roads, rail or airports which bring visitors.
5 Name its main towns. How large are they (in population, etc.)?
6 What are the key attractions of the Lake District?

National parks

Study pages 226-227 of the textbook for 5 minutes. Focus on Figure 4 on page 227 and have an atlas with you to check which towns and motorways are which. Close the atlas.

Revision activities

1 From memory, name the eleven National Parks in England and Wales.
2 Without looking at the atlas, do activity 3b in the textbook.
3 Suggest reasons why the Peak District is the most visited National Park in England and Wales.

Figure 4 The Lake District National Park

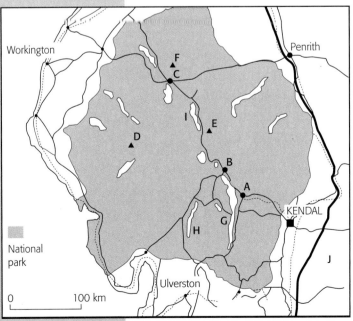

The Lake District National Park

Revision activities

The following activities refer to pages 228-229 in the textbook. If you've studied another National Park, use the same kinds of activities for that one.

1 Figure 4 shows a sketch outline of the Lake District National Park. Name the following:
   a the towns lettered A, B and C
   b the mountains D, E and F
   c the lakes G, H and I
   d motorway J.
2 Add labelled arrows showing where motorway J leads (a) to the north, (b) to the south.
3 What are the names of the three main rock types in the Lake District? Shade these in on Figure 4.

Which motorway would you use to travel to the North, out of London? • Which is the highest peak in England?

The landscape of the Lake District N P

This page refers to pages 230-231 of the *It's a World Thing* student textbook.

Revision activities

1 Landscapes depend on past and present processes, and also a mixture of natural and human processes.
  a Draw an A4-sized copy of Figure 5. Make the boxes large enough to write in.
  b Then, using pages 230-231 of the textbook, label and give examples of how rock type, past processes and human activities have all made the landscape what it is today.

If you have not studied the Lake District National Park, you should still do this exercise, but for your own case study.

Figure 5 Factors affecting the landscape

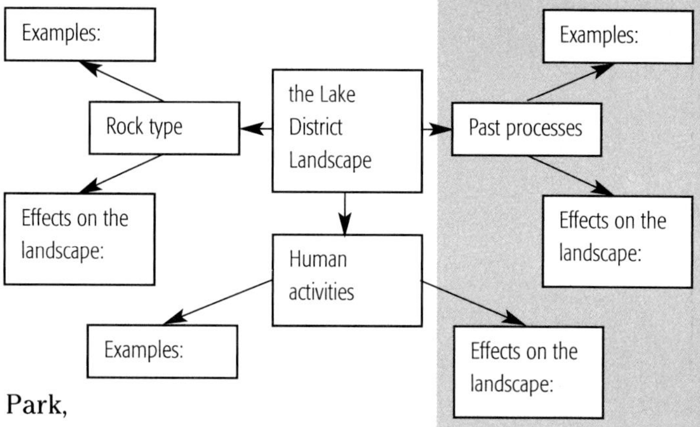

Examples:

Rock type → the Lake District Landscape → Past processes → Examples:

Effects on the landscape:

Human activities

Effects on the landscape:

Examples:

Effects on the landscape:

Revising mapwork

The following activities use the Ordnance Survey (OS) map extract, Figure 3, on page 231 of the textbook. You should be familiar with grid references, direction, distance and scale, because examiners are free to ask about these. The key to the map is on page 246 of the textbook. You should do these activities even if you have not studied the Lake District National Park as your case study.

Revision activities

1 Give the four-figure map references for the following:
  a the town of Ambleside (the buildings, not the name);
  b the small lake called Rydal Water.
2 Name and give six-figure grid references for:
  a three peaks over 450 metres in height;
  b two places where a 'B' road joins an 'A' road;
  c two car parks.
3 How far is it (i) in a straight line and (ii) by road, between:
  a the hotels in Skelwith Bridge and Elterwater?
  b the Drunken Duck Inn (351013) and the hotel in Grasmere (337074)?
4 In which direction does:
  a Ambleside lie from Skelwith Bridge?
  b Grasmere lie from Ambleside?
  c Raven Crag (3908) lie from Ambleside?
5 Study Figure 4 on page 231 of the textbook. It shows why people like the Lake District National Park. Then close the book.
  a Name 3 things people like most about the Lake District National Park.
  b Which outdoor activity is named in the chart?
  c How many headings in the chart are to do with the landscape itself?
  d How many headings are about the peace and quiet of the Lake District?

Name three lakes in the Lake District. • On a 1:50 000 map, how far does 4 cm represent in km?

Managing conflict in the Lake District National Park

This page refers to pages 232-241 of the textbook. Although the activities refer to the Lake District, you can apply them to any National Park which you have studied, in the UK or overseas.

Figure 6 Costs and benefits of tourism

Benefits	Interest groups affected, and how they are affected
■ Sale of produce ■ Employment ■ Income from B&B in converted barn ■ A ■ B ■ C ■ D	■ Local farmers because …
Costs	
■ Traffic congestion ■ Traffic noise and air pollution ■ High house prices ■ E ■ F ■ G ■ H ■ I	■ Young people, low-paid workers, elderly because …

Revision activities

Conflict occurs in the Lake District, as in all National Parks, because different users want different things. These activities focus on conflict resulting from **honey-pots**.

1 Study Figure 6. It shows some costs and benefits resulting from tourism.
    a Make an A4-sized copy of the table.
    b Add as many other benefits (letters A – D) and costs (letters E – I) as you can think of.
    c Fill in the column for the interest groups affected and how they are affected. Two have been started for you.
2 'Tourism brings more problems than benefits'. What do you think? Write bullet-point notes for a 6-mark answer to show what you think about this statement. Remember to use examples.

Conflict in the Lake District NP

This section refers to pages 238-241 in the textbook.

Revision activities

The following activities are about the conflict about speedboats on Lake Windermere in the Lake District National Park.

1 For the following interest groups, explain why they are for or against the speed ban. Write one sentence per group.
    ■ Ambleside and District Anglers' Association
    ■ Cumbria Wildlife Trust
    ■ South Windermere Sailing Club
    ■ Friends of Windermere
    ■ Holidays Afloat
    ■ Waterhead Marine Ltd
    ■ Windermere and Bowness Chamber of Trade
    ■ Windermere Water-ski Association
2 Now complete a conflict matrix, for these groups. You should refer to page 241 of the textbook to help you.
3 What solutions are possible for this issue? Can everyone be happy?

What is a honey-pot? ● Why might an environmentalist not want speedboats on Windermere?

Eco-tourism in LEDCs

This page refers to pages 242-245 in the *It's a World Thing* student textbook. If you have studied another eco-tourist study, use the same exercises because you can adapt them easily. Before you start this exercise, try this quick quiz:

1 What is eco-tourism?
2 What is sustainable development?
3 Name four indicators that show Zimbabwe's poverty.
4 What's the difference between 'preservation' and 'conservation'?
5 For your chosen LEDC, list the tourist attractions that take holidaymakers there.

The background to eco-tourism

Zimbabwe is one of the world's poorest countries, but it possesses huge assets in its scenery, climate and wildlife. The textbook shows how local people can improve living standards by taking control of how these assets are managed.

Revision activities

Read the information about Zimbabwe on page 242 of the textbook. Focus on learning Figure 3 (the map of Zimbabwe), Figure 2 (the 'Factfile') and the text. Spend 10 minutes on this. Then close the book.

1 Study Figure 8 and do the following.
  a Name countries A, B, C and D.
  b Name river E, lake F, and river G.
  c Name cities H and J.
  d Name two of the six national parks.

2 Figure 9 shows socio-economic data about Zimbabwe. Each has three options, one of which is correct. Circle the correct one.

3 Zimbabwe's poverty is because of which of the following statements? Tick those which are true, and correct those which are false.
  a 62% of the country is poor-quality land.
  b 42% of the land is poor and supports 50% of the population.
  c The poorest land has low rainfall and thick forest.
  d Cattle ranching is the only viable economic activity in the poorer lands.

4 Now read through page 243 in the textbook. Summarise what eco-tourism involves by making a list of activities run by local people and their benefits.

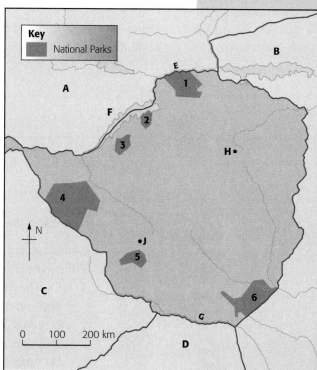

Figure 8 Map of Zimbabwe

Figure 9

	Option 1	Option 2	Option 3
Income (GNP) per person per year in US$	1035	240	540
Life expectancy (years)	51	48	63
Literacy (% of men / women)	70/80	80/90	90/80
Population (million people)	13.7	12.4	11.4
Population increase (each year)	1.7%	2.7%	3.7%
% of population living in rural areas	59%	69%	79%

How might the present political climate in Zimbabwe affect tourism? • Which nearby countries offer similar attractions to Zimbabwe?

Tourism in LEDCs: the ups and downs

Revision activities

Look at the issues in Figure 10, which explain some of the general pros and cons of tourism in LEDCs. Some are social, whilst others are economic or environmental.

Figure 10

Foreign currency is brought into the country.	Natural environments are lost with the construction of airports, roads and hotels for tourists.
There is pressure from mini-buses in popular game reserves.	There is a greater variety of ways to earn income for the country's population.
Farmland is taken away for game parks.	Visitor numbers have fallen in recent years.
Most jobs created by tourism pay low wages.	Crops often get eaten or flattened by wildlife.
Only a few local people gain employment in tourist activities.	Many service-sector jobs become available, such as in hotels, cafes and transport
Improved services result from tourism, e.g. roads, water and electricity.	Jobs provided in tourism are often seasonal.
Craft industries develop to satisfy tourist demand.	More jobs in traditional villages reduces rural-urban migration.
Farmers have a market for their products.	Local customs, traditions or dress survive only as attractions for tourists.

1 **a** Write the letter A beside the **two** greatest benefits for the nation's economy.

  b Write the letter B beside **five** benefits for local people in tourist areas.

  c Write the letter C beside **two** environmental issues or problems presented by tourism.

  d Write the letter D beside **three** conflicts most likely to arise between tourists and local people.

  e Write the letter E beside **three** economic problems that could arise in the local area.

2 Make an A4-sized copy of Figure 11 below. On it, write down the following statements in the correct box.

  ▨ Permits granted to tour companies allow local people to gain income.
  ▨ Local people decide whether or not hunting should take place.
  ▨ Less crop damage is caused by limiting elephant numbers.
  ▨ Former poachers may become tour guides.
  ▨ Villagers can host tourists.
  ▨ Local people have changed their attitude to wildlife.
  ▨ Land is controlled by local communities.
  ▨ Income from permits in communities has led to new services, such as schools and health care.
  ▨ Trophy hunting is a valuable low-volume, high-income tourist attraction.
  ▨ Conservation of wildlife is now practised by villagers (e.g. hunting quotas).
  ▨ Land is now sometimes fenced off.
  ▨ Local people can sell handicrafts and souvenirs.

Figure 11

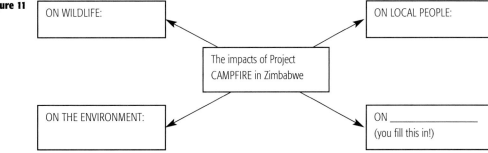

ON WILDLIFE:

ON LOCAL PEOPLE:

The impacts of Project CAMPFIRE in Zimbabwe

ON THE ENVIRONMENT:

ON _____
(you fill this in!)

Is local tradition and culture ruined by tourism? ● Do tourists raise the expectations of locals too high?

What words do I have to know?

There is no set list of words in the specification that you must know. However, examiners will know that you have probably used the set textbook, and will feel free to use some or all of the following words in the examinations:

accessibility	conservation	footpath erosion	leisure	mobility	seasonal	traffic pollution
conflict	diversification	geology	licences and quotas	National Park	employment	trophy hunting
congestion	eco-tourism	honey-pots	management	relief	sustainable tourism	vegetation

The glossary in the student textbook will help you with the meanings of several of these words and phrases.

What other sources can help me?

National Parks in the UK

a   http://www.anpa.gov.uk (Association of National Park Authorities)
b   http://www.breconbeacons.org
c   http://www.dartmoor-npa.gov.uk
d   http://www.pembrokeshirecoast.org.uk
e   http://www.eryri-npa.co.uk (Snowdonia)
f   http://www.peakdistrict.org
g   http://moors.uk.net (North York Moors)
h   http://www.yorkshire-dales.com
i   http://www.lake-district.gov.uk
j   http://www.hants.gov.uk/newforest
k   http://www.lochlomond-trossachs.org
l   http://www.exmoor-nationalpark.gov.uk

Sustainable or eco-tourism in an LEDC

The Global eye website has good material on a number of schemes such as CAMPFIRE in Zimbabwe and others in Malaysia, Belize and Ecuador:
http://www.globaleye.org.uk

Try these questions

1   Describe the conflicts which have arisen due to the popularity of your chosen National Park. What management solutions are there for these conflicts? (*6 marks*)

2   Describe an eco-tourism project in a named **LEDC** that you have studied. What have its benefits and problems been? (*6 marks*)

Case-study answers

These two pages will help you to understand what examiners are looking for in terms of case studies. The question which these examples refer to was set by Edexcel Examinations in June 2003, Paper 4H. It was part of question A2 on Settlement and Employment, worth 8 marks.

The case-study question

'You have studied employment patterns in a town or city in an MEDC. Explain how the local council and businesses are attracting jobs and customers back into the CBD of that town/city.'

The question requires the candidate to:

a name a town or city. Make sure you do this, because, if you don't, the maximum mark available would be 5 marks.

b name an MEDC city – not an LEDC city! You would be surprised how many candidates misread the question. If you named an LEDC city, you would gain no more than 2 marks.

For your case study in *'It's a World Thing'*, the town of Reading would be an ideal example to choose.

The mark scheme

The mark scheme is in three levels, from Level 1 (lowest) to Level 3 (highest). Examiners are looking for a balanced answer with detail rather than a list of points.

Level 1	1-2 marks	The answer mentions a few simple developments, describing what has happened to either employment or shopping, but does not say how people have been attracted back specifically. It lacks detail. For example: "The shopping area has been modernised and more car parks have been built."
Level 2	3-5 marks	The answer describes a few developments in some detail. For example: "X street was pedestrianised, Y car park was extended". It mentions something about both employment and shopping, and one or two ways in which people have been attracted back. One or two points are well developed. For example: "People prefer the new Oracle shopping centre because it is under cover. It offers jobs, too, such as shop managers and security staff".
Level 3	6-8 marks	The answer is a clearly explained account, with detail which balances both shopping and employment. It also makes clear how the council and/or businesses have tried to attract people back. Most or all parts of the answer are well developed, i.e. they give more detail about **what** happened, **where**, and **why**. For example: "The local council redesigned X and Y streets into pedestrian precincts to make these safer for shoppers by keeping traffic away"; "A new park-and-ride scheme for shoppers was planned by the council at X to avoid traffic congestion in the centre of town and to make it safer".

Try marking these!

Two responses from candidates who sat the exam are given on page 96. Read through both and try to decide (**a**) which level each candidate is reaching, and (**b**) what mark you would give them within that level. The marks awarded to these candidates are given at the end of page 96 – but don't look at them until you've assessed the answers yourself! The answers are provided exactly as they were originally written, spelling and punctuation included. You don't need to mark the quality of the language because this is given a separate mark at the end of your exam paper.

Answer A *Name of local town or city = Bromley*

Approximately ten to fifteen years ago, the Glades Shopping Centre was built in Bromley Town Centre. After Bluewater shopping centre was built near the Dartford Tunnel in 1995, it has been Bromley's main competitor. In order to win back customers and employment, Bromley's council had to do some new things. The Glades introduced late night shopping on Thursdays until 8 o'clock and some new shops were built. The construction of Waitrose the supermarket and the new Police Station was completed in order to improve the appearance of Bromley South. During the summer, the council arranged for certain activities to be held in the High Street for example French markets, Scottish dancing, carisell, trampolines, and in the winter there are traditional Christmas markets, in order to attract customers. There are also plans to open a leisure centre complex at Bromley South.

Answer B *Name of local town or city = Reading*

Local councils and businesses have made many changes to Reading over recent years. All have contributed to making Reading a busy and popular place to be. One main attraction is the football stadium, which was once a very small arena, to small to accommodate the large number of fans the Reading Royals FC had. Fans were getting crushed due to no seating and metal bars getting in the way. The club needed a new stadium to be upgraded to the 2nd division, so the Madjeski Stadium was soon built. It holds many more people than the old one, and includes seats. There has also been a hotel and leisure centre built near-by for people visiting. It was built outside the CBD where business parks have recently been built, and to make Reading more pleasurable a new shopping centre was added. It is very large with upmarket stores for Readings increasing population.
A lake runs through it which makes it a pretty place to be. Due to this centre emplyment is readily available, and a good night life makes people want to be part of the CBD of Reading.

What marks did you give?

Answer A

This was a fairly strong answer. It makes it clear who made the decisions to enable Bromley to compete and what needed to be done. If anything, it spends too long on this – the first three sentences!

It does say **what** happened and **where**, e.g. late night shopping was started and some new shops were built at the Glades shopping centre; a Waitrose supermarket was built at Bromley South; summer activities and traditional Christmas markets were held in the High Street; a leisure centre complex has been planned for Bromley South.

However, it doesn't really explain **why** this has happened, apart from winning back customers and improving the appearance of Bromley South. It says very little about employment – it is mainly about shopping.

Answer B

This answer has been included so that you can see a problem answer. Did you spot it? It's deceptive because there is a lot about the Madjeski Stadium and developments in football! But all of this – as you will know if you have studied Reading – is on the **outskirts** of the town. Only the last part of the answer is relevant. Studying the question would have helped this candidate. **Beware that you don't make the mistake of misreading the question as well.**

Only the following things are relevant about **what** has happened: a new shopping centre, upmarket stores, and a lake have been built. "Night life" is too vague a description to be useful.

Little, if any, explanation about **why** is given, except for Reading's increasing population. Employment is mentioned but not specified.

The examiners awarded the following marks:
Answer A - a medium Level 2 mark of 4 out of 8.
Answer B - a basic Level 1 mark of only 2 marks.